THE ART OF BECOMING

A MORAL BLUEPRINT FOR GENERATION ALPHA

VOLUME THREE

EWURAMMA HANNAH BOAH

THE ART OF BECOMING
VOLUME THREE

ISBN: 979-8-9913042-1-4

Copyright © 2026 by EWURAMMA HANNAH BOAH

Contact Author on:
Mobile: +1 (646) 701-1905
E-mail: cbdcministries.org@gmail.com

Layout Design by:
INDES PROCOM LIMITED
Phone: +233 20 800 0464
Email: info@indesprocom.com

Cover Design by:
Richard O. Agyeman
Co-Founder/Creative Director
Acute Formula LLC

ENDORSEMENTS

AS A TEACHER FOR MANY YEARS, I AM OFTEN ASKED how to prepare students for the future. We speak of academics, skills, and opportunities. Rarely do we speak of resilience, faithfulness, and purpose as foundational pillars of character. This book does.

It shows that integrity is infrastructure, resilience is renewable energy, purpose is navigation, and faithfulness is maintenance. Without these, even the brightest student burns out. With them, ordinary students become luminous.

The chapters on resilience and purpose should be mandatory reading in every secondary school. They are not motivational clichés; they are strategic frameworks for sustainable growth. This is not inspiration for a moment. It is formation for a lifetime.

Benedicta Kakra Bentil
Special Education Teacher,
New York City Department of Education
Master of Science in Education (M.Sc.Ed)

THIS BOOK SPEAKS WITH CLARITY, WISDOM, AND HEART. As a teacher, I witness daily the challenges students face, navigating comparison, expectations, fractured friendships, and quiet struggles. Rarely do I encounter a work that addresses their world while lifting their gaze higher. This one does.

The prose is lyrical without indulgence. The wisdom is firm without harshness. The vignettes feel authentic, not imagined. I could see my students in Kwame, Naana, Hannah, and Kojo, and I could also see their future, steadier, stronger, if they internalize the lessons within these pages.

Awards may honor its craftsmanship. Time will honor its truth.

Rose Otchere
Special Education Teacher,
New York City Department of Education
Master of Science in Education (M.Sc.Ed), Dual Certification,
12 Years of Service in Special Education

FOR FIFTEEN YEARS, I HAVE DEDICATED MYSELF TO guiding students through challenges, triumphs, and the quiet work of becoming. I have seen brilliance flourish when grounded in integrity, and I have seen promise falter when direction and purpose were absent. This book speaks to the essential lessons that often go untaught, the inner curriculum of character, discipline, and resilience.

This is more than a book; it is a guide to shaping a life. It constructs understanding with intention, lays foundations of moral judgment, opens doors to wisdom, strengthens the structures of responsibility, and furnishes the mind with tools for thoughtful action. It reminds us that education is complete only when knowledge is transformed into formation.

What impressed me most is its companionship with the reader. It does not lecture from afar. It acknowledges struggle, cultivates curiosity, and calls students to rise without shame or fear. In a world overflowing with distraction and noise, this book restores moral clarity and empowers conscience to speak.

It deserves a place in classrooms, on bookshelves, and in the hands of young people determined to live with integrity. Its insights are timeless, its guidance practical, and its message necessary.

Eric Ato Apronti
Special Education Teacher,
New York City Department of Education
Master of Science in Special Education (M.Sc.Ed)

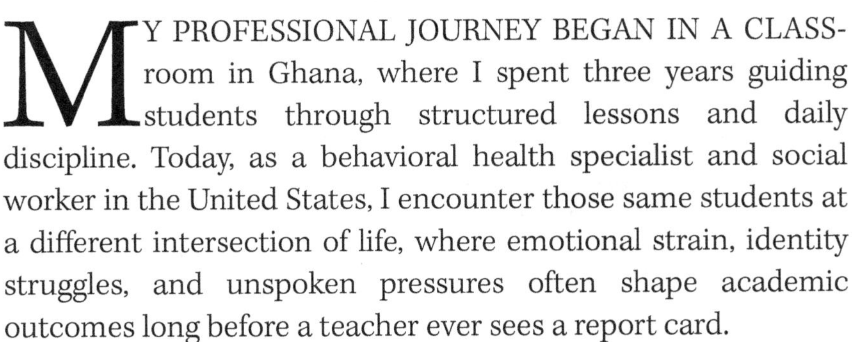

MY PROFESSIONAL JOURNEY BEGAN IN A CLASS-room in Ghana, where I spent three years guiding students through structured lessons and daily discipline. Today, as a behavioral health specialist and social worker in the United States, I encounter those same students at a different intersection of life, where emotional strain, identity struggles, and unspoken pressures often shape academic outcomes long before a teacher ever sees a report card.

Across five years in behavioral health and two years working directly with students in social work practice, I have learned that the greatest barriers to success are rarely intellectual. They are internal. They are relational. They are matters of character and conviction.

This book addresses those hidden dimensions with remarkable precision. It does not speak at young people; it speaks into the spaces they quietly wrestle with. It understands the tension between potential and pressure. It names the influence of relationships with clarity. It distinguishes loyalty from faithfulness in a way that is both timely and necessary in our cultural moment.

What resonates most with me is its balance. It challenges without shaming. It corrects without humiliating. It invites reflection without creating fear. In my work, I see the long-term consequences when guidance comes too late or not at all. This manuscript offers that guidance early, before patterns solidify and before wounds deepen.

From the vantage point of both educator and mental health practitioner, I can say with confidence that this is more than an inspirational read. It is a formative resource. It belongs in schools, counseling spaces, youth programs, and homes. Its impact will not be momentary; it will be generational.

Mary Nketiah
Behavioral Health Specialist 5 years)
Social Worker supporting students 2 years
Master of Social Work (MSW)
Diploma in Education; Former Classroom Teacher, Ghana 3 years

DEDICATION

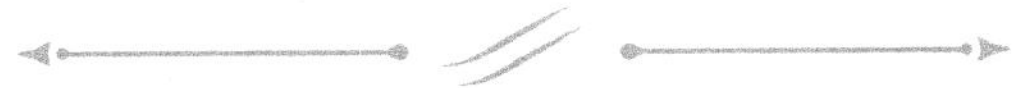

THIS BOOK IS LOVINGLY DEDICATED TO MY DEAREST friend, Nana Adwoa Bemah Agyemang-Badu, a devoted teacher at Accra Academy, and through her, to teachers everywhere across the continents, in crowded classrooms and rural schools, in underfunded districts and well-resourced academies, in villages, cities, and places history forgets to name.

Before I ever set foot on the sixth-form campus, Providence was already at work on my behalf. Through what seemed like an ordinary crossing of paths, my aunt encountered Adwoa and discerned in her something rare. Out of that meeting, a friendship was arranged for me before I even knew I needed one. It is not common for someone to entrust their child to another young person with such confidence, yet my aunt saw in Adwoa a steadiness of spirit and a reliability of heart, and she placed me under that covering. What I would later recognize as divine foresight began as a simple introduction.

Though we were both young, Adwoa carried herself with a maturity that surpassed her years. A Yaa Asantewaa girl, she was a lady at ease in her own skin, neither intimidated by others nor dependent on their approval. There was a quiet strength about her, a composure that never demanded attention but always commanded respect. In our friendship, she assumed a posture that felt almost maternal.

As the daughter of our Assistant Headmaster, Adwoa watched over me without controlling me. She guided me without diminishing me. She noticed the small things that revealed vulnerability and responded with care rather than ridicule. When I struggled with meals in the dining hall, she ensured I was provided for from the Assistant Headmaster's quarters. She never publicized her kindness, she simply made sure I was sustained. It was not merely the food that nourished me but the intention behind it, the unspoken assurance that I was seen and that I mattered. Her friendship became a covering over my formative years.

On weekends, although we had juniors assigned to serve us, Nana would personally wash our uniforms, our vests, and even our socks. She did not delegate what she considered care. She knelt where others might have claimed entitlement. In those quiet moments, dignity was redefined for me. Leadership, I learned, was not proven by being served but by serving. Her hands did more than cleanse fabric; they reinforced love, humility, and responsibility. Those simple acts carried a theology of character I would only later understand.

Because of the quiet honor attached to her position as the Assistant Headmaster's daughter, I was granted a measure of influence I might not otherwise have possessed. That proximity allowed me to uphold and share the morals and etiquette I carried within my soul from my previous school, guiding and inspiring those around me.

In Adwoa, I came to understand that fidelity is not merely a sentimental virtue but a sacred one. It is the deliberate and unwavering choice to remain, to stand, to uphold truth, and to sustain friendship when convenience would suggest retreat. Through her example, I learned that trust is the silent architecture of every enduring bond, and fidelity is its foundation. What she embodied in friendship, she now practices in her profession.

As an educator, she carries into the classroom the same constancy she lived as a friend. Her commitment to her students reflects the integrity of her character. She teaches not only with knowledge but with presence. She offers not only instruction but stability. In a world that often celebrates talent more than loyalty, she has shown me that faithfulness is the higher gift. Through her life, I have witnessed how character precedes influence and how consistency quietly shapes destinies.

Her leadership has since been recognized beyond the classroom. She now serves as School Counselor of Accra Academy, entrusted with the emotional and moral guidance of students navigating some of the most formative years of their lives. She is also the SU Patron, shepherding spiritual growth and accountability among the students, and the Patron of the SRC, mentoring young leaders in responsibility and integrity. In addition, she contributes her voice and wisdom as part of the School Management, helping shape the governance and direction of the institution. These roles are not merely titles, they are extensions of the same fidelity, steadiness, and moral clarity she embodied long before any formal recognition followed.

And so, in honoring Adwoa, I honor every teacher who quietly becomes shelter and strength to those entrusted to them. This dedication extends beyond one friend to all who arrive before the first bell and remain long after the corridors fall silent. It recognizes those who carry lesson plans in one hand and invisible burdens in the other. You do more than deliver content, you cultivate character, steady trembling confidence, and shape souls in ways statistics can never measure.

You stand daily at the intersection of potential and becoming. You witness the fragile space where curiosity wrestles with fear, where brilliance hides behind distraction, and where courage flickers until it becomes flame. In that sacred space, you make decisions that influence not only academic outcomes but the direction of lives.

You are builders of futures you may never personally see fulfilled, architects of character in a generation that tests every foundation placed before it. You steward questions that seldom appear on examinations, questions of identity, integrity, belonging, and purpose. While society measures performance, you measure growth and protect dignity. When the surrounding culture grows loud and restless, you cultivate discernment and steady thought.

Your work requires strength that is rarely applauded. You correct without crushing. You challenge without humiliating. You hold standards without surrendering compassion. You choose patience over frustration, presence over indifference, and formation over mere information. You believe in possibility, even when belief is faint in the student standing before you.

This book is dedicated to your endurance and unseen labor. It is dedicated to the quiet authority you carry and the moral courage required to remain faithful in a profession that asks much and often thanks little. May these pages serve you as you have served generations. May they strengthen your resolve when the work feels heavy and remind you that no investment in a young life is ever wasted.

The world is shaped in your classrooms more than history books will ever admit. Your consistency strengthens communities. Your influence steadies families. History itself bends toward the seeds planted by teachers who refuse to give up. And eternity alone will reveal the full measure of all your faithfulness has built.

With enduring gratitude, this work stands as a small return for all you have sown.

FOREWORD

SOME BOOKS INFORM. OTHERS INSPIRE. A RARE FEW build. This is a book that builds.

We are living in an age of acceleration. Movement is celebrated more than meaning. Visibility is rewarded more than virtue. Young people are taught how to perform before they are taught how to become. In such a climate, talent blooms early but often withers under pressure. Momentum is abundant. Direction is scarce.

This work enters that tension with unusual clarity and moral steadiness.

What distinguishes this book is not merely its urgency but its architecture. It does not scatter advice like seeds on concrete. It constructs a life. Identity is laid as a foundation. Integrity rises as inner structure. Relationships open as doors. Resilience becomes the roof that withstands storms. Purpose fills the rooms with meaning. Faithfulness sustains daily habitation. The metaphor is not decorative; it is formative. By the final chapter, the reader is no longer gathering tips. The reader is inhabiting a design.

The brilliance of this manuscript lies in its restraint. It does not rely on alarmism, nor does it romanticize youth. It dignifies young people by assigning them responsibility. It assumes they are capable of greatness, not the loud and viral kind, but the enduring kind. The kind forged in private decisions, in small obedience, in returning the coin, rebuilding the failed experiment, finishing the assignment, keeping the promise.

In a distracted generation, this book teaches depth.

In a divided generation, it teaches discernment.

In a fragile generation, it teaches resilience without hardness.

In an ambitious generation, it teaches purpose without vanity.

The stories woven throughout are not ornamental. They are anchors. A lemonade stand becomes a legacy. A windmill becomes light. A piggy bank becomes wells. A quiet student becomes a pillar. These narratives are not fairy tales but evidence that character compounds, that steady faithfulness reshapes communities, that suffering rightly stewarded can outlive empires.

Most striking is the book's moral balance. It distinguishes loyalty from faithfulness, perseverance from resilience, motion from meaning. It recognizes the digital pressures unique to Generation Alpha without demonizing the age they inhabit. It teaches young people how to move through algorithms without surrendering their souls. It invites them not to withdraw from the world, but to build straight within it.

This is what gives the book its timelessness. It addresses contemporary storms with ancient wisdom. It speaks in modern cadence while echoing truths older than civilization: integrity extracts respect, unity multiplies strength, purpose steadies the heart, faithfulness outlasts applause.

The world does not suffer from a lack of intelligence. It suffers from a lack of inner coherence. We have engineered extraordinary technologies while neglecting the architecture of the human spirit. This book answers that neglect. It restores formation as education's forgotten pillar. It insists that before a young person can lead a movement, build a company, heal a nation, or shape a culture, they must first learn to govern themselves.

Awards may one day honor its craftsmanship. Institutions may adopt it as a curriculum. Parents may place it in trembling hands before graduation ceremonies. Yet its truest success will not be measured in accolades but in lives that remain steady when storms arrive, in relationships that choose unity over rivalry, in leaders who finish what they begin, in adults who remember that greatness is not spectacle but structure.

If you are a teacher, this book will give language to lessons you have long carried.

If you are a parent, it will offer a blueprint for roots that hold through shifting seasons.

If you are a young reader, it will not flatter you. It will fortify you.

Enter these pages not as a spectator but as a builder. Read slowly. Reflect deeply. Construct intentionally. The future will not belong to the loudest generation. It will belong to the one who learned how to build.

Bernard Aboagye *(PhD, MSc,*
BSc, AEE, AEPG, CSEMP)
Department of Mechanical Engineering
Sunyani Technical University
Sunyani, Ghana, West Africa

PREFACE

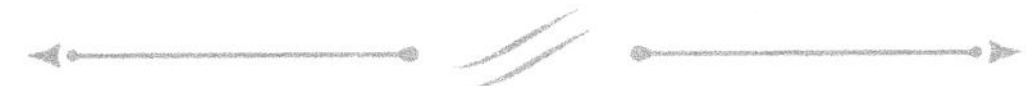

ON AN ORDINARY DAY, MY WORLD STOPPED.

There was no earthquake. No headline announcing catastrophe. No siren sounding a national emergency. It was simply a young Ghanaian man, barely older than I had once been as a sixth former, seated before a camera. He spoke with confidence. Then he insulted the President of the Republic of Ghana and his wife.

Not disagreement. Not principled dissent. Insults. Mockery. Contempt.

Something shifted within me. My eyes filled with tears, not because leaders are beyond criticism, but because something deeper had moved beneath the surface of our culture. In that moment, two Ghanas stood before me. One loud and unrestrained, intoxicated with visibility. The other disciplined and reverent, formed by restraint and guided by an inherited code of honor.

I remembered the Ghana that formed me.

We stood when elders entered a room, not because we were forced, but because respect had been woven into us before we understood its language. We greeted neighbors as Auntie and Uncle, because community was assumed rather than negotiated.

Correction required only a look. A raised eyebrow carried more weight than a lecture.

Respect was not performance. It was posture.

Discipline was not oppression. It was preparation.

Restraint was not weakness. It was strength under control.

A quiet question began to follow me: What happened to our culture?

That question traveled with me across years and continents. America has been generous to me. It has offered opportunity, order, and room to grow. For that, I am grateful. But gratitude does not cancel responsibility. Exposure does not erase origin.

As I observed both worlds, the one that raised me and the one that refined me, I noticed a subtle erosion. Honor, dignity, humility, and self-restraint were increasingly dismissed as relics of a slower age. Noise was replacing wisdom. Confidence was replacing humility. Visibility was replacing depth.

History teaches that cultures do not collapse overnight. They erode gradually through attitudes tolerated, through language excused, through standards lowered one degree at a time. Erosion rarely announces itself. It disguises itself as modernity.

Silence would have been easier. Silence would have been comfortable. Silence would have been wrong.

This book is not nostalgia. It is responsibility. It is my response to a question that would not release me. It is my refusal to watch erosion and call it progress.

I believe restoration is possible. I believe honor can return. I believe dignity can return. I believe integrity, respect, and trust can be rebuilt. But restoration will not come through complaint or longing for the past. It will rise through deliberate men and women who choose character over convenience, restraint over applause, substance over spectacle.

This book exists because silence would have been easier and wrong.

ACKNOWLEDGEMENTS

I BEGIN WITH PROFOUND GRATITUDE TO GOD, MY first Teacher, my constant Guide, and the source of all wisdom. Before any classroom, before any syllabus, before Sunday school lessons or secular instruction, He shaped my heart, guided my steps, and planted seeds of understanding that have grown throughout my life. Every lesson of integrity, every principle of character, every truth I now hold and share in these pages is rooted in His patient, unwavering instruction.

To Him, I owe the first words I learned, the first lessons I lived, and the foundation upon which all other learning has been built. His guidance has been quiet yet steadfast, gentle yet unyielding, calling me to truth, discipline, and purpose at every stage of my journey.

I am deeply grateful to the Sunday school teachers who poured themselves into my life with patience and care. Their dedication nurtured my understanding of faith, instilled moral clarity, and showed me the value of living according to principle. Their stories, prayers, and gentle corrections left a lasting imprint that continues to guide me today.

To my secular teachers, I owe recognition for shaping my intellect and curiosity. Each lesson, each challenge, and each expectation taught me more than academics; they taught resilience, focus, and the courage to pursue excellence even when the task seemed difficult. You did more than teach; you modeled discipline, wisdom, and the rewards of consistent effort.

To mentors and guides beyond the classroom, whose insight and encouragement illuminated paths I might not have seen, I offer sincere thanks. Your counsel reminded me that learning extends beyond textbooks and lectures; it lives in relationships, decisions, and the courage to act rightly when circumstances are uncertain.

Finally, I thank my family, friends, church, and community for their support, encouragement, and accountability. You reminded me that education, character, and purpose are never solitary pursuits; they are cultivated in the soil of shared care and mutual growth.

Each person mentioned, each life intersected, has contributed to the architecture of my journey. To God be all glory, for every lesson, every guide, every teacher, and every challenge that led to this work.

Ewuramma Hannah Boah

TABLE OF CONTENTS

A NATIONAL MANIFESTO

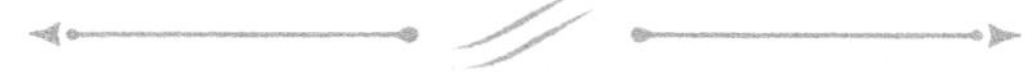

TO THE YOUNG AND RISING GENERATION:

You were born at a hinge moment in history. Never before has a generation held the world in the palm of its hand. With a single device, you can access centuries of accumulated knowledge. You can learn languages, build businesses, explore sciences, and engage global conversations. With that same device, you can absorb distraction, imitation, comparison, and corrosion.

Knowledge has never been more accessible. Noise has never been more relentless.

Wisdom will not grow by accident. It must be planted, practiced, and protected. Every young person must carry a clear vision of who they intend to become five, ten, twenty years from now. Not a fantasy shaped by applause, but a vision shaped by purpose.

When you know who you are becoming, your behavior aligns with it. You do not insult for attention. You do not exchange your name for relevance. You do not drift through education, work, and relationships without direction.

There must come a day when you convene a private meeting with yourself and ask whether your life aligns with your vision, where you drifted, and what must be corrected. That private meeting may be the most consequential gathering of your life.

This book is part of that planting. Its lessons are drawn from builders, men and women who began with little and constructed something lasting through discipline, skill, patience, and persistence. They are steady. They are reliable. They are the quiet architecture beneath functioning communities.

Character compounds. Skill multiplies. Discipline pays.

Certificates are valuable. Degrees are useful. Titles are honorable. They are not enough. Degrees alone will not heal corruption. Titles alone will not rebuild trust. Income alone will not restore dignity. Strong men and women of character will.

To the Ghanaian at home and abroad:

You are not detached observers of national life. You are bridges. Whether you rise in Accra, Bangkok, Cairo, Dublin, Edinburgh, Florence, Geneva, Hanoi, Istanbul, Jakarta, Kumasi, Takoradi, or in the heart of our local markets, your exposure is not accidental. You have witnessed what accountability produces. You understand what discipline and structure can build.

Your success is entrusted influence.

Ask how what you have learned can strengthen Ghana. Ask how your experience can fortify the next generation.

Place this book into the hands of every Junior High School final-year student preparing to enter Senior High School. Not as charity, but as strategy. Those students stand on a narrow bridge between adolescence and adulthood. The habits formed there will follow them into universities, workplaces, marriages, leadership, and public life.

If we reach them before cynicism does, shape them before indifference does, fortify them before corruption tempts them, we do not merely inspire individuals. We alter trajectories. We influence history.

Sponsor copies. Adopt schools. Adopt districts. Adopt regions. Let no student cross into Senior High School without holding a blueprint for discipline, vision, integrity, and responsibility.

History will ask what we did when we recognized erosion. Let it be said that we responded. Let it be said that we invested. Let it be said that we rebuilt.

The work of restoration does not belong to one author. It belongs to a people.

Now, let us build deliberately and courageously together.

PART THREE

01

AUTOMOBILE SERVICE

*The Young Person Who Keeps People
Moving Safely*

A Conversation with Generation Alpha

MODULE I — The Door That Wouldn't Open

"CHARLIE, HOW?" You already know that question. Not curious. Not cruel. Just careful.

You wrote WASSCE. You prayed hard. You refreshed the portal again and again, morning, afternoon, and night.

Your friends are shouting: "Legon, here I come!" "KNUST loading!" "Tech, we move!"

Your own screen says: "No program offered."

Your aunt says, "Rewrite." Your uncle says, "Try nursing." Someone laughs, "You go and learn fitting."

It stings.

Because in your mind, fitting means dirty overalls, grease, noise, shouting, and people quietly concluding that you didn't just fail an exam, you failed life.

Then one afternoon, your father's car refuses to start. No warning. No mercy.

A young mechanic arrives barely older than you. Tablet in hand. Clean jumpsuit. Quiet confidence.

He plugs in a scanner. Checks. Listens. Reasons. Thirty minutes later, the engine hums back to life. Your father pays him more than some office workers earn in a day.

And as you drive home, he murmurs, almost to himself, "If this boy stays serious, he will never be hungry."

Something flickers in your chest.

Maybe this is not what people do when school fails. Maybe this is engineering in motion. Maybe this is dignity wearing overalls. That tension between disappointment and possibility is where our journey begins.

MODULE II — The Garage That Felt Different

Accra, 7:05 a.m.

Kwesi pulls into a modest service station, half-hidden beside a pharmacy. He is tense. Late for a presentation. His car jerks at every red light.

He expects grease and guessing. Instead, courtesy meets him.

An attendant wipes his hands and says, "Good morning, boss. What is the car doing?"

Not "What's wrong?" But "What is it doing?"

Kwesi explains. The attendant listens carefully. Repeats the details. Notes his schedule.

A specialist scans the car. Another listens to the engine's rhythm. Within minutes, they find the fault: a failing sensor and a clogged filter.

"We can fix it," the attendant says calmly, "but it will take an hour. Take one of our small cars for your meeting."

Kwesi blinks. "How much extra?"

"Nothing. It's part of the service."

He returns later to find his car ready, the steering wheel wiped, the tyres checked, and the bill clear.

No tricks. No rush. Just care.

Driving away, he realizes something quietly but firmly: this is how professionalism should feel.

MODULE III — When "Just Manage It" Becomes Dangerous

Across the country, drivers share one famous phrase: "Just manage it."

The brake feels soft. The steering drifts. The engine coughs.

We raise the radio. We hope. Sometimes it works until it doesn't.

A small leak becomes engine damage. A missing bolt becomes an accident.

Automobile service exists because "just manage it" is not a plan.

Lives depend on knowledge, not luck.

Skilled technicians stand in that space between fear and failure and say: "Let's find the real fault. Let's fix it properly. Let's prevent the next one."

MODULE IV — When Service Becomes Rescue

Kumasi. Evening rain drizzles on the ring road.

A family returns from church. The father has postponed brake repairs for weeks.

A trotro cuts in front. He slams the pedal. The car slows barely. They stop with hearts pounding. He drives straight to a quiet workshop he once ignored.

No lectures. No blame.

The young technician simply says, "Let's check it."

They lift the car. Pads gone. Discs scored. Brake fluid is dark The technician explains clearly. Offers options. Even a payment plan. They work late. By night's end, the car stops cleanly again.

The father whispers, "I should have come sooner."

The technician replies, "Next time, listen fast."

That is service: not repair alone, but protection.

MODULE V — What Technicians Actually Do

Automobile service is applied engineering with a heartbeat.

Technicians diagnose electrical, electronic, and mechanical systems; maintain engines, brakes, suspensions, steering, and transmissions; use scanners, software, and multimeters; keep records; explain faults in plain language; and make decisions that directly affect lives.

They work in roadside bays, branded dealerships, fleet yards, inspection centres, and teaching labs. Every day, they combine science, honesty, and discipline so wheels keep turning safely.

MODULE VI — The Discipline Of "Courtesy Plus"

Years ago, one garage built its reputation on a simple creed: Courtesy Plus.

They refused tips. They wiped the steering wheels. They warned customers before faults grew. They followed up two weeks later: "Are you satisfied? We are here if you need us."

They spent money on services others ignored and earned trust that money couldn't buy. Because good service always returns as loyalty.

MODULE VII — Is This Path For You?

Ask yourself: Do machines and moving parts fascinate you? Do you enjoy discovering why something works or doesn't? Can you stay patient when a problem hides? Do you care about people's safety? Can your hands and mind cooperate under pressure?

If yes, this might be alignment, not punishment.

MODULE VIII — The Cost And The Training

Automobile service demands more than muscle. It asks for physical effort and precision, integrity when tempted, and humility to keep learning.

In Ghana and globally, training begins at apprenticeships and NVTI/TVET programs, technical institutes and polytechnics, and automotive engineering courses at universities. Short courses are available in diagnostics, hybrid systems, AC repair, and mechatronics. Vehicles evolve. So must you. Knowledge protects you and those who trust your skill.

MODULE IX — Reward Beyond Money

Automobile service gives steady income and self-reliance, skills that travel anywhere wheels turn, deep satisfaction, the joy of solving what once confused, and respect that grows quietly through consistency.

You may not get applause. But every safe journey will whisper your name in gratitude.

MODULE X — The Moment You Understand Why

Every true technician remembers the day a stranded family reached home because you stayed late, the driver who said, "Since you fixed it, it hasn't failed once," the repair you refused because it could have killed someone.

Those memories become medals no school can give.

FINAL WORD — Standing Where Machines Fail, and People Trust

Automobile service is more than work. It is stewardship. Each bolt you tighten declares: someone's life matters. Each honest diagnosis preserves a future journey.

A well-repaired brake is as holy as a well-preached sermon; both can save lives. So if you choose this path, not because you failed, but because you see truth in it, then you are not doing fitting.

You are standing where machines fail and people trust. You are keeping a nation moving. And that is sacred work.

BUILDING CONSTRUCTION

*For Generation Alpha in Ghana and
Across the World*

THE SILENT ARCHITECTS

EVERY GENERATION CELEBRATES VOICES. FEW celebrate hands. Statues are raised to speakers. Rarely to builders. Yet when speeches fade and regimes collapse, walls remain standing. This chapter is not an argument. It is a revelation.

MODULE I — The Work That Holds The World Together

There are many learned people in the world, but some remain the least among their peers not for lack of knowledge, but for lack of usefulness. Some gather degrees yet remain strangers to the practical duties of daily life. Some study the relics of antiquity yet neglect the living needs of the present. Some master dead languages yet cannot build anything that helps the living.

Far better is the learning that serves. Far greater is the knowledge that builds. Civilization stands on three needs: food, clothing, and shelter. And of these three, shelter is the one every human being depends on every single day.

Before a doctor can heal, a teacher can teach, a judge can judge, a pilot can fly, a president can lead a builder must build. Remove builders from history and civilization never begins.

Generation Alpha must understand this truth early: the building construction trade is not merely a job. It is the backbone of civilization.

MODULE II — Mark At The Reunion: The Question That Stopped Laughter

At his senior high school reunion, Mark the boy with eight As once destined for medicine stood quietly among doctors, lawyers, and engineers. "What do you do now?" they asked. "Building construction," he replied. Silence followed.

"Construction? That's for ordinary people. You were meant for greater things." Mark met their gaze and asked, "Do you mean to say God is ordinary?"

The atmosphere shifted. "He built the heavens, the earth, the mountains, and the seas. When I raise a wall, I continue His craft. Without builders, where would your brilliance sleep?" The room fell quiet.

Purpose does not always wear suits. Sometimes it carries a trowel. Laughter is loud until truth enters the room. Then silence does the speaking.

MODULE III — Opoku Anim: From Jobless To Skilled And Secure

Opoku Anim graduated with an HND in Marketing in 2018 and faced years of unemployment in Ahafo until Newmont Ghana Gold offered construction training. In three months, he earned certifications in welding, fabrication, and steel bending alongside seventy-five other youth.

Today, he works on the Ahafo North Project. He supports his family. He plans his future. He sleeps without fear of tomorrow. No university degree was required. Skilled hands proved more valuable than unused qualifications.

Opoku's story teaches a quiet truth: Success is not always loud. Sometimes it is steady, reliable, and built with your own hands.

MODULE IV — The Land Demands Builders

Look around your community. How many new buildings have risen in the past year? How many schools are overcrowded? How many hospitals need expansion? How many families need homes?

Visit the nearest construction site and observe: excavators carving foundations, masons laying stone with precision, steelworkers framing the future, carpenters, plumbers, electricians bringing walls to life.

Cities like New York and Detroit once ran half-day schools because buildings were insufficient. Across Ghana, entire villages rise daily yet thousands more skilled hands are needed. Food and clothing sustain life. But shelter protects it.

If the land cries out for builders and you are alive in that moment, the calling is not mysterious.

MODULE V — God Built First

"In the beginning, God created..." Genesis 1:1. Bezalel was filled with the Spirit to build the Tabernacle   Exodus 31. *"Unless the Lord builds the house..."* Psalm 127.

Before God spoke to prophets, He built a world for them to stand in. Every cathedral, classroom, and clinic traces its origin to His hands. Builders do not choose ordinary work. They choose divine imitation.

Generation Alpha, understand this: Dusty boots can carry sacred purpose.

MODULE VI — Masonry: Foundation Of Civilization

Masons built pyramids that still stand, Roman roads that endure after 2,000 years, and ancient tombs that defy time. Modern masons build: foundations, skyscraper casings, chimneys and fireplaces, fountains and walkways, arches and stone walls.

A mason does not rush. He builds for people he may never meet.

MODULE VII — Plasterer: Interior Beauty's Architect

Plasterers transform rough walls into smooth canvases. They shape ceilings, curves, and surfaces with precision and artistry. Beauty is not decoration. It is part of human dignity. Civilization pays for beauty because beauty shapes how people live.

MODULE VIII — Structural Steel Worker: The Sky's Trusted Hands

Steelworkers frame the tallest structures. They walk where the air thins and the ground disappears. The sky trusts only the steady.

MODULE IX — The Full Construction Corps

A building is not a miracle. It is coordination. From contractor to landscaper, from architect to electrician, from mason to painter more than a hundred specialists must work in harmony for any structure to stand. Construction is not one trade. It is a nation of trades.

MODULE X — The Young Adult Career Ladder

SHS → Skilled Professional → Supervisor → Contractor.

Level 1: Entry (3–6 months): Newmont Construction Training, TVET certificates (masonry, carpentry, plumbing), NVTI Levels 1–2.

Level 2: Specialist (1–3 years): Mason, Steelworker, Plasterer, Welder, Electrician. Salary: GH¢2,500–6,000 monthly.

Level 3: Foreman/Supervisor (3–7 years): Lead 20-man crews. GH¢8,000–15,000 monthly.

Level 4: Contractor (7+ years): Own a company. Build schools, hospitals, estates. GH¢50,000+ monthly revenue.

This ladder is not theory. It is walked daily.

MODULE XI — Why Construction Outlives Titles

Some careers chase applause. Others create the platforms applause stands on. Construction is: recession-proof, future-proof, globally needed, locally respected, financially stable, spiritually meaningful.

The world needs thinkers. But it also needs builders and builders are thinkers.

MODULE XII — The World War Building Famine

When building stops, society bleeds quietly. After World War I, families were homeless, schools ran half-day, and cities struggled to recover. Modern Ghana builds entire communities in months yet the demand for skilled builders continues to grow.

MODULE XIII — Apprenticeship: The Mason's University

Three years transform boys into masters: Year 1: mortar, bricks, observation. Year 2: rough walls, plumb, level. Year 3: finishing, curves, artistry. Apprenticeship is humility with a future.

MODULE XIV — The Moral Reordering Of Work

The world measures success by title. God measures it by what remains standing. History does not remember who spoke the loudest. It remembers what endured.

MODULE XV — Every Hand Mirrors God's Hand

God did not study medicine, argue law, or crunch numbers. He built. When you lay a brick, you echo His precision. When you raise a wall, you extend His mercy. When your building shelters families, you continue His work.

Dusty boots can carry divine purpose. Calloused hands can wield sacred tools.

FINAL WORD — Your Hands Were Made For This

Stand before any skyline at dusk. Every silhouette is a builder's signature. Generation Alpha your hands were not made for smallness.

If you choose this path, you are not choosing "a trade." You are choosing to hold up the world. You are choosing to build what will outlive you. You are choosing purpose.

And purpose, unlike buildings, never collapses.

03

CARPENTRY: PRECISION CRAFT, NOT COMMON LABOR

*For Generation Alpha in Ghana and
Across the World—SHS/JHS Graduates*

THE SILENT PRECISION

EVERY GENERATION CELEBRATES THE LOUD. FEW honor the exact. Speakers fill auditoriums. Carpenters frame them. Presidents cut ribbons. Carpenters build the stages. When applause fades and lights dim, wooden beams remain silent witnesses.

SHS/JHS graduates: Your hands were born for this.

MODULE I — John Harrison: The Carpenter Who Outsmarted The Scientists

John Harrison was not a university graduate. He was not a mathematician. He was not an astronomer. He was a carpenter's son.

At age 20, while others figured out life, Harrison turned his Yorkshire workshop into a precision laboratory no metal gears, only oak and lignum vitae. By 1730, he solved the impossible: H1-H4 marine chronometers ended 200 years of shipwrecks by cracking longitude.

Astronomers failed for centuries. One carpenter succeeded. Parliament's £20,000 prize (millions today) fought him 40 years. King George III intervened. H4 triumphed 1761 Jamaica voyage.

Truth: The boy who whittles wood outsmarts universities.

MODULE II — The Modern Carpenter: Planner, Designer, Genius

Carpenters don't hammer blindly. They calculate before cutting. Harrison measured seconds across oceans. Your carpenter measures millimeters for doorframes. Same brain. Different scale.

What elite carpenters master:

1. Plans buildings (sketches → homes)
2. Calculates lumber (exact board feet)
3. Estimates costs (market prices)
4. Selects wood (perfect grain match)
5. Frames structures (load-bearing skeletons)
6. Builds scaffolding (sky safety)
7. Modern tools (concrete/metal integration)

8. Building codes (legal mastery)
9. Team coordination (plumbers/electricians)
10. Portfolio building (Instagram = CV)

Interview your local carpenter. SHS math becomes real.

MODULE III — Mark's Reunion + Harrison's Proof

"Do you mean God is ordinary?" Mark asked. John Harrison answered with H4. Both rejected "greater things": Doctors heal bodies → Carpenters frame clinics; Pastors preach → Carpenters build pews; Presidents lead → Carpenters stage them.

SHS 8-As dilemma: Medicine OR divine carpentry? Harrison chose wood. Changed history.

MODULE IV — Kofi Mensah: JHS Dropout → Sawmill King

Kofi Mensah: JHS complete, no SHS fees. 2024: Church carpenter apprentice (GH¢800 + food). 2026: Kumasi church framer, 12-man crew, sawmill owner (GH¢4,000 monthly). No HND. No Newmont. Wood + discipline. JHS hands > empty certificates.

MODULE V — Why Carpentry Never Dies

Last year in your town: New roofs counted? Churches needing pews? Schools deskless? Homes doorless? World Wars: Buildings stopped. Families homeless. Carpenters rebuilt nations. AI era: Robots weld. Machines write. No machine frames family homes.

Global demand: Ghana, UK, US, Canada carpenters travel with skills as passports.

MODULE VI — Carpenter's 7 Sacred Calculations (SHS Math Lives)

Your classroom formulas find purpose:

1. Lumber volume: Length × Width × Thickness
2. Board feet: (Thickness × Width × Length) ÷ 12
3. Cost: Market price × Quantity
4. Waste: +10-15% buffer
5. Load: Roof weight × span ÷ support
6. Angles: Trigonometry (roofs/stairs)
7. Openings: Doors + windows = material balance

Harrison: Seconds across Atlantic. You: Millimeters for perfection. Same genius.

MODULE VII — 6 Woods Dominion (Ghanaian Mastery)

Wood lives raw. Dies without carpenter:

WOOD	STRENGTH	USE	PRICE
Mahogany	Luxury grain	Doors/furniture	High
Teak	Weatherproof	Outdoor eternal	Premium
Odum	Bulletproof	Structural beams	Local
Emire	Beauty king	Fine furniture	Medium
Rosewood	Precision rich	Instruments	Export
Pine	Affordable	Mass framing	Entry

MODULE VIII — Cabinetmaker: Wood's Poet

Framing pays bills. Cabinetry builds dynasties. Elite crafts: Chippendale chairs (GH¢20K replicas), Sheraton tables (elegant geometry), piano casings (musical sculpture), staircase art (function + poetry), mansion paneling (wall wealth).

Machine can't match: Hand-cut dovetails, flawless grain flow. Income: GH¢6K-15K monthly.

MODULE IX — SHS/JHS → Carpenter Millionaire (Exact Timeline)

Level 1: Apprentice (6-12 months)

- Church/market master carpenter
- Saw/planing/joinery basics
- GH¢800-1,500 + food/meals
- Portfolio: Stools → shelves

Level 2: Journeyman (1-3 years)**

- Independent house frames
- Furniture profit center
- GH¢2,500-5,000 monthly
- Tool investment: GH¢10K target

Level 3: Foreman (3-5 years)**

- 8-12 man leadership
- GH¢7,000-12,000 monthly
- Truck ownership: GH¢80K

Level 4: Contractor (5+ years)**

- 50+ workers, churches/schools
- GH¢40K+ monthly revenue
- Sawmills + permanent shops

Kofi Mensah walked it. You can.

MODULE X — Carpenter vs Office: Reality Check

CARPENTER	OFFICE JOB
GH¢2.5K → own boss	GH¢1.5K → 15 years servitude
Recession-proof	Layoff roulette
Global passport	Local cage
Harrison → millions	Degree → applications
God-called craft	Man-made title

MODULE XI — Slack Season = Profit Season

Winter slow? Elite pivot: Furniture (indoor cashflow), cabinetry (mansions), repairs (neighborhood steady), pattern-making (factory gold), boat building (coastal premium). Smart carpenters earn 2X in "slack."

MODULE XII — 12 Tools Arsenal (GH¢5k Startup)

1. Crosscut saw (timber mastery)
2. Jack plane (surface perfection)
3. Chisels set (joinery precision)
4. Try square (90° truth)
5. Spirit level (plumb law)
6. 10m tape (SHS math)
7. Claw hammer (force control)
8. Bar clamps (pressure perfection)
9. Marking gauge (line eternity)
10. Workbench (stability throne)
11. Oil stone (edge immortality)
12. Toolbox (mobile kingdom)

Harrison built H4 with less.

MODULE XIII — The Carpenter's 10 Eternal Laws

1. Measure twice, cut once (SHS discipline)
2. Grain direction = strength (wood wisdom)
3. Season properly (crack prevention)
4. Joints > nails (true strength)
5. Plumb absolute (building law)
6. Customer vision first (repeat wealth)
7. Clean site always (professional mark)
8. Sharpen daily (speed secret)
9. New joint yearly (master evolution)
10. Build for grandchildren (legacy law)

MODULE XIV — Cabinetmaker Millionaire Path

Framing = survival. Cabinetry = dynasty. Elite revenue streams: Mahogany sets: GH¢15K profit each, teak wardrobes: GH¢8K margins, office paneling: GH¢25K contracts, church pulpits: GH¢12K prestige.

Machine shops fail: Hand-dovetails, grain perfection. Austria Master: Fine work = wealth. Mass production = skill death.

MODULE XV — God The Carpenter, You His Apprentice

Harrison solved longitude. God shaped universe. Scripture proof: Genesis 2:7 "God formed man" (carpenter hands), Exodus 31 Bezalel Spirit-builder, Matthew 13:55 Jesus "carpenter's son."

Your dovetail = God's fingerprint. Roof truss = heaven's geometry.

FINAL WORD — JHS/SHS Hands Change History

Raise your right hand, Generation Alpha: "My hands mirror God's hands. I solve oceans with wood. Carpentry over certificates. Harrison over Harvard. Yɛn Ara Asaase Ni."

John Harrison: Died millionaire age 83. Kofi Mensah: Employs 25 age 28. Your first plank awaits.

Two roads diverge: Office cage + CV spam OR Wood dust + world-changing craft. Ghana's cathedrals need framing. Your plane answers. What will you build?

04

ELECTRICIANS, PLUMBERS & PAINTERS: HANDS THAT BUILD CIVILIZATION

The Silent Builders Of Comfort, Health, and Beauty

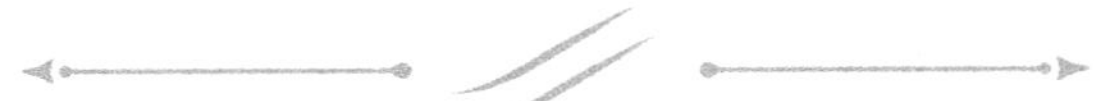

NANCY WATCHED AS A LADDER CREAKED UNDER Kwame's hands while he rewired the classroom by sunset, the lights shone brighter than the Accra sun. Every glowing home, flowing tap, and vibrant wall exists because of hands often overlooked.

Electricians light cities. Plumbers bring life. Painters make spaces breathe. Without them, homes are dark, cold, and dull. With them, life flows, shines, and sings.

Gen Alpha reminder: Your hands can shape comfort, health, and beauty.

MODULE I — John Goffe Rand: The Painter Who Freed Color

(One Tube Changed Art Forever)

London, 1841. A weary portrait painter scrapes dried pigment from a brittle pig's bladder. The paint is ruined his week's work lost. Out of frustration, he engineers a small metallic tube sealed with a screw cap.

That painter was John Goffe Rand, and his invention the collapsible paint tube revolutionized art itself. It: Preserved oil paints for months. Set painters free to capture sunlight in the open air. Made possible the luminous strokes of Monet and Renoir.

Renoir confessed, "Without tubes, there would be no Impressionism."

Gen Alpha lesson: One creative irritation can generate a movement. One painter's problem freed color for the planet.

MODULE II — Thomas Crapper: The Plumber Who Protected Millions

(Pipes Are Life)

Yorkshire, England. A craftsman bends copper under a rain-damp roof, shaping what will one day save cities from disease. Thomas Crapper (1836–1910), master plumber, brought modern sanitation to life:

Invented the floating ballcock, preventing overflow. Perfected the U-bend trap, blocking deadly sewer gas. Opened the first bathroom showroom, earning royal warrants. His work reduced cholera and preserved royal palaces.

Gen Alpha lesson: Pipes are not just tubes they are arteries of public health.

MODULE III — Frank Julian Sprague: The Electrician Who Electrified Cities

(Sparking Civilization's Heartbeat)

On a Navy ship, a young electrician dreams of moving entire cities by current instead of steam. Frank Sprague (1857–1934) made that dream real.

1884: Invented the first practical electric streetcar motor. **1888:** Powered Richmond, Virginia's 12-mile electric trolley 40 cars running flawlessly. Over 200 patents followed: streetcars, elevators, subways, regenerative braking.

By 1900, his systems ran in 438 cities. Humanity's rhythm changed forever.

Gen Alpha lesson: Electricians don't fix wires they spark civilization's heartbeat.

MODULE IV — Modern Painters: Beyond Color, Into Civilization

(Color Protects & Inspires)

A painter today is both chemist and artist. Exterior: Weatherproofs homes, resists Ghana's rains and dust. Interior: Colors wards and classrooms, turns cement into comfort. Skills: Mix pigments accurately, test under tropical light, maintain health and safety. Career: Apprentice → Expert → Contractor → Brand Owner.

Case in Ghana: Abena Boateng, JHS graduate from Kumasi started as church apprentice at 17, now leads hospital and school projects, earning GH¢35K+ monthly by 24.

Gen Alpha lesson: Paint is more than decoration it is protection, identity, and hope on walls.

MODULE V — Modern Plumbers: Silent Protectors

(Sanitation Saves Nations)

Plumbers keep civilization alive every second. They: Install water and gas systems, heating lines, sewage drainage. Prevent contamination, flooding, backflow, disease. Read blueprints, test pressure, and maintain purity.

Example: Yaw Antwi, plumber from Tamale, built 15 rural clinic water systems before age 25 today runs a sanitation enterprise serving seven districts.

Gen Alpha lesson: Every clean faucet, hospital tap, and toilet bears the invisible signature of your skill.

MODULE VI — Modern Electricians: Power Architects

(Energy Is Destiny)

Electricians turn darkness to data, silence to sound, stillness to enterprise. They: Power hospitals, airports, schools, and solar plants. Wire smart homes and factories. Design safe, efficient energy networks.

Example: Kwame Mensah, Accra electrician, wired Ghana's first student-built solar classroom. At 23, his team now installs green systems nationwide.

Gen Alpha lesson: Energy is destiny and your circuit completes the nation's heartbeat.

MODULE VII — Tools, Techniques & Gen Alpha Math

(Hands + Brains = Civilization)

Painter: Brushes, rollers, ladders, color-mixing stations. **Plumber:** Pipe wrenches, torches, spirit levels, testers. Electrician: Wire strippers, voltage analyzers, conduit benders.

Science = profit: Paint coverage = area × coats. Water flow = diameter × pressure. Power load = volts × amps.

Hands + brains = cities, homes, and hope.

MODULE VIII — Career Timeline: Apprentice → Master → Owner

(From First Job to Mega-Projects)

Level	Duration	Role	Income (GH₵)	Outcome
Apprentice	6–12 mo	Learn tools & safety	800–1,500	Build portfolio
Journeyman	1–3 yrs	Handle independent jobs	2,500–5,000	Gain reputation
Foreman	3–5 yrs	Lead 5–12 workers	7,000–12,000	Manage teams
Contractor	5+ yrs	Own company	25K–50K+	Run mega-projects

Remember: Rand, Crapper, Sprague—all began at Level 1.

MODULE IX — Trades vs Office: Reality Check

(Skills > Certificates)

TRADE	OFFICE JOB
Builds cities & homes	Sends emails that vanish
GH¢2.5K → 50K+ monthly	GH¢1.5K → 15 yrs servitude
Recession-proof	Layoff roulette
Skill = passport	Certificate = application
Hands change history	Paperwork gathers dust

Gen Alpha truth: Trades are civilization's foundation. Offices rest upon them.

MODULE X — God, Creation, And Craft

(Divine Hands in Human Hands)

Painter → Color = Creation. Plumber → Flow = Life. Electrician → Energy = Civilization.

Scripture proof: Genesis 1: God painted creation with light and sky. Exodus 31: Bezalel filled with the Spirit of craftsmanship. Matthew 13:55: Jesus, the carpenter's son, dignified manual work forever.

Your hands mirror God's. Every brush stroke, pipe joint, or circuit line leaves a divine fingerprint on earth.

The Final Builder's Creed — Generation Alpha, Your Hands Build Nations

(Start Small, Build Forever)

Nations rise not on speeches but on skilled hands. When your wiring lights a newborn's first cry, or your paint dresses a classroom in hope, you are no mere laborer you are a nation-builder.

Raise your right hand and declare: "My hands create beauty. I light homes, run water, and color life. Trades over certificates. Rand over stagnation. Crapper over disease. Sprague over darkness."

Your first tool awaits.

Two paths lie ahead: The office cage of endless CVs. The creative frontier of wires, water, and color where your hands forge tomorrow.

Mini Challenge for Today: Pick one: a brush, a wrench, or a tester. Transform a single wall, pipe, or circuit in your home. Small hands, big nation.

Which will you choose?

FARMING

*The Young Person Who Wanted
to Feed a Future*

A Conversation with Generation Alpha

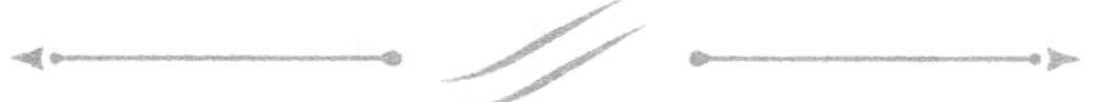

MODULE I — When The Mind Won't Cooperate

SOME YOUNG PEOPLE FAIL EXAMS BECAUSE THEY never learned. Kojo was not one of them.

He attended classes. He stayed for extra lessons. He copied notes carefully. He prayed before every paper.

Still, on exam days, the words on the page scattered. Formulas slipped. Comprehension passages floated past his understanding. His teachers said, "You are trying," but results said otherwise.

Family noticed. His mother woke him early to study with him. His cousin offered to "coach" him for free. The youth leader brought up past questions and circled topics to focus on.

Everyone wanted to help. But Kojo's brain felt like a door that opened slowly for others and stubbornly for him.

He was not lazy. He was tired of trying and still watching his scripts come back with marks that didn't match his effort.

So when people started suggesting paths in security work, shop assistant, or "small job" in town, he heard another sentence behind their words: "You're not a book person."

One afternoon, an uncle visiting from the village said quietly, "Your mind may not like long paragraphs. But your hands, your eyes, your patience, they may be hiding your real intelligence."

Kojo did not argue. He only asked, "So where does someone like me stand?"

MODULE II — A Letter From Uncle George

Weeks later, a letter arrived from an older relative, Uncle George, a farmer who had spent his life between fields and books.

Dear Nephew,

I hear from your mother that you are a thoughtful boy, and that school is not treating you as kindly as you had hoped. I am glad you are thinking carefully about your next steps. I'd hate for you to regret a decision taken in anger or shame.

Many think farming is for those who "could not manage" books. They forget that a good farmer calculates, observes, records, and decides. He must know soils, crops, animals, markets, and people.

A shop may close when the owner travels. A farmer's work continues while he rests: plants keep growing, animals keep feeding, soil keeps changing. The question is not, "Is farming easy?" It is, "Are you willing to learn with your hands, eyes, and mind together?"

Do not rush. Think. But remember: land does not reject a person who works it honestly and wisely.

Yours for a wise decision,

Uncle George.

Kojo folded the letter. He had always assumed "real intelligence" belonged to classrooms. Uncle George was suggesting something dangerous and freeing: that another kind of intelligence might fit him better.

MODULE III — William Kamkwamba: When Curiosity Outruns English

Malawi, 2002. A village swallowed by drought.

A teenage boy, William Kamkwamba, watched his family's maize dry and crack. School fees could not be paid. He had to leave the classroom behind.

But his mind kept asking questions. He found an old science book about windmills in a small library. The English was hard. Diagrams became his teachers.

He studied the pictures again and again: blades, shafts, gears, a pump. He went to a scrapyard and collected broken bicycle parts, PVC pipes, old tractor parts, and a dynamo.

People mocked him. "William's madness," they said. He kept building.

One day, the wind blew. The blades turned. A bulb lit the first electric light in his home. Later, a pump pulled water. Their field no longer waited helplessly for rain.

William did not "pass an exam" to become important. He combined curiosity with scraps and changed his family's future.

His story travelled the world not as a story of a "bush mechanic," but of an inventor, a farmer, a problem-solver.

Kojo read about William and thought, "So somebody who struggled with English text used diagrams to save a farm. Maybe my difficulty in one place is not the end of my mind—just a sign to learn differently."

MODULE IV — First Furrows: Kojo Tests The Ground

The chief in Kojo's town had heard about his situation and Uncle George's letter. One evening, after a community meeting, the chief called him aside:

"There is unused land near the stream," he said. "Not a gift, an opportunity. Start small. If you work it well, we will see."

Kojo's heart pounded. He was scared of failing again this time, in front of everyone. But he remembered: how textbooks confused him, how practical demonstrations in school agriculture class made sense, how he felt strangely calm when working with his hands.

He did not take all the land. He started with half an acre. Onions and peppers. Something simple. Something people needed every day.

His new "classroom" became: the texture of soil in his fingers, the way plants leaned toward light, the speed water disappeared from mounds, the notes he scribbled in a small exercise book: dates, rainfall, growth.

The first season was not a miracle. Pests came. Some rows failed. Old farmers shook their heads. But some beds thrived. He sold his first harvest in small bowls and baskets, with small profits but honest.

At night, instead of homework he did not understand, he read MoFA bulletins, short articles on spacing, mulching, compost, and simple charts on soil nutrients.

It was the first time learning felt connected to his body and his day.

MODULE V — Farming As Vision, Not Punishment

Farming is not what people do when "brains fail." Farming is what nations do when they take their future seriously.

It is: food security, applied science, climate strategy, logistics and storage, engineering in the open air, business and negotiation, community life, and national planning.

Every school meal, hospital diet, factory lunch, restaurant plate depends on someone who once knelt in the soil and decided: "I will understand this land and work with it."

Modern farming uses: soil tests and lab reports, drip irrigation and sprinklers, weather apps and satellite images, greenhouses and shade nets, improved seeds and careful organic matter, data on pests, yields, and prices.

It is not an excuse for people who "can't read." It is a stage where a different kind of reading takes place of clouds, leaves, soil, and numbers.

MODULE VI — What Farmers Actually Do

Good farmers are: observers, experimenters, planners, and negotiators.

They test soil before planting, choose crops that match rainfall and market conditions, rotate fields so the land does not "wear out," manage pests without destroying future fertility, plan harvests to hit better prices, and store and transport carefully so food does not rot before it is sold.

One careful soil test before tomatoes can save a whole season's income. This is not guesswork. It is science with consequences.

MODULE VII — The Wisdom of Diversification

Uncle George wrote of farmers in his time who learned the hard way: one crop + one bad year = disaster.

Some farmers in the American South built a statue to the boll weevil, the insect that destroyed their cotton and forced them to diversify. They later discovered that "enemy" saved their community from poverty by pushing them into new crops.

The principle is simple and timeless: One crop is fragile. Many crops are protection.

Wise farmers combine: maize with vegetables, cassava with plantain, poultry with crops, goats with grass fields, tomatoes with peppers and onions.

So that if rain delays, a pest targets one plant, or price crashes for a single crop, something else still stands.

Diversification is not just old farming wisdom. It is risk management, a kind of insurance written in seeds instead of paper.

MODULE VIII — Is This Your Alignment?

This path is not for everyone. Ask yourself: Do practical tasks calm you more than long theory? Do you enjoy watching things grow and change? Do you notice small details in outdoor shade, moisture, and leaf colour? Does the idea of "building something living" appeal to you? Can you keep going even when results take months, not days?

If your brain feels heavy in some classrooms, but wakes up during practical work, that is not stupidity. That may be calling.

Farming is not "the only thing left." It might be the one thing that finally fits.

MODULE IX — The Cost of This Calling

Farming is honest work. Honesty includes admitting it is hard.

It demands: early mornings and late evenings, sweat under sun and rain, losing some crops and starting again, learning from people who may not respect your age at first, and keeping records even when you are tired.

You will face: buyers who want low prices, seasons when fertilizer is expensive, and pests that do not respect your effort.

If this makes you afraid, be truthful. If it makes you afraid and still interested, pay very close attention.

MODULE X — Training For The Land

You do not need a PhD to farm well. But you do need training.

Learning can come through: SHS agriculture classes, TVET or NVTI programmes, agricultural colleges and universities, short courses in irrigation, poultry, and greenhouse systems, MoFA extension officers and farmer field schools, and online videos and radio programs on best practices.

You can specialize in: crops (vegetables, cereals, roots), livestock or poultry, greenhouse production, irrigation design and maintenance, agribusiness and processing (turning produce into products).

Your tools are not only a hoe, a cutlass, and boots, but also a notebook, a simple calculator, and a phone with a weather app and price updates.

Knowledge is the farmer's sharpest cutlass.

MODULE XI — What This Work Gives Back

Farming gives: visible results from your effort, a skill that travels wherever seeds can grow, a measure of independence from office clocks, respect from the people you quietly feed, and a chance to improve land instead of exhausting it.

You may never trend on social media. But you may be the reason a community never goes hungry.

MODULE XII — Kojo's Second Report Card

Years later, Kojo received something that felt like a new kind of result slip. It was not from WAEC. It was from life.

Restaurants called weeks in advance for his vegetables. Neighbours asked him to train their children. MoFA officers took pictures of his fields to show at workshops. A bank officer visited, not to chase debt, but to offer a small facility for expansion.

He still could not solve some past exam questions. But he could: read his soil, plan his seasons, negotiate fairly, and feed hundreds.

Kojo finally understood: His brain had not been broken. It had simply been built for a different classroom.

FINAL WORD — Feeding A Future

Farming does not exist to explain your "failure." It exists to feed futures.

It is the decision to turn bare ground into food, confusion into systems, rejection into service. If you walk this road, not because school closed its doors, but because you see truth and fit in it, then you are not "just farming."

You are sustaining life. You are protecting tomorrow. You are shaping a nation quietly.

Your hands are instruments. Your mind is the tool.

Will you let the land become the classroom where your real intelligence finally stands up?

06

FORESTRY

MODULE I — Imagine a World Without Trees

CLOSE YOUR EYES. PICTURE A PARK WITH NO TREES. Bare ground. No shade. No birds singing. No swings hanging from branches. What do you see? Empty. Sad. Hot.

Now open your eyes. Trees give us oxygen, shade, fruit, medicine, timber, and beauty. Without them, our world would feel naked.

Look around: The chair you sit on, the floor beneath your feet, your books and notebooks, paper bags, cereal boxes, barrels, furniture, all of these once came from trees. Forests provide us with lumber, pulp, and countless other materials that shape daily life.

Fun Fact for Gen Alpha: One mature tree produces enough oxygen daily for four people to breathe. About 90% of paper comes from wood pulp, even your school books were once part of a tree.

Reflection Prompt: Make a list of everything you used today that came from trees.

MODULE II — When Pages Blur But Trees Speak Clearly

Some Gen Alpha kids struggle with books. Words dance. Numbers hide. Exams feel like mountains. But put them in a forest, and something clicks.

Sena noticed patterns others missed: When the air felt different after rain, when a tree leaned slightly more than last week, when soil cracked earlier than usual, when birds changed their flight patterns.

During a school cleanup under a tall teak tree, she whispered, "If this tree weren't here, this whole place would feel wrong." Her teacher smiled. "You're seeing what most people walk past."

Reflection Prompt: When have you noticed something in nature that others ignored? How did it make you feel smart?

MODULE III — Ghana's Forest Guardians

Across Ghana, young forest rangers and entrepreneurs protect woodlands from chainsaws and fire, turning barren hills green again. They started small: patrolling community forests on foot or by motorbike, teaching villages sustainable timber harvesting, planting native species like mahogany, iroko, and shea, and guarding against illegal logging and bushfires.

Challenges hit hard: Poachers working at night, droughts cracking the soil, conflicts over "free" firewood. But they persisted.

Today, many lead teams restore hundreds of hectares each

year, supply sustainable timber to markets, create jobs through eco-forestry, and share progress on community radio and WhatsApp groups.

Did You Know? Ghana lost 60% of its forests since 1900, but rangers plant 30 million trees each year to fight back!

Reflection Prompt: If you found a forest edge being cut illegally, what's your first step to protect it?

MODULE IV — Kwame Bonsu: The Ghanaian Entrepreneur

In the Afram Headwaters Forest Reserve, Kwame Bonsu refused to accept that degraded land must stay degraded. Through Ghana's Forest Investment Program (2015–2024), he received support in 2021 to restore part of the reserve.

His Strategy: Teak plantations for long-term timber income, 20,000+ mango trees for medium-term returns, traditional crops for immediate cash flow.

His Results: 180+ local jobs created, improved crop yields for 11 rural communities, reduced deforestation, sustainable income streams, and restored forest reserve where wildlife and people thrive.

"I want to get the forest back. But it's also about improving the quality of life for rural communities, the people who depend most on the forest."

Kwame's story shows Gen Alpha: You can restore land, build wealth, create jobs, protect the planet, and start small and grow big.

MODULE V — Trees As a Classroom

Forestry isn't "bush work." It's science, math, and stewardship combined. A forester masters: Soil testing and seedling growth, fire prevention and trail mapping, timber estimation using geometry, disease control and insect scouting, community education, and conflict resolution.

Forestry is: Climate work, national security work, and environmental justice work.

MODULE VI — Timber & Non-Timber Wealth

Timber (odum, emire, teak) becomes: School desks, church pews, market stalls, bridges, export furniture. Skilled foresters ensure: Selective cutting, mature trees only, replanting after every log.

Non-Timber Forest Products feed without killing trees: Shea butter, honey, mushrooms, snails, medicinal herbs, rattan crafts, charcoal from deadwood.

Fun Fact: One mature mahogany tree can yield timber worth GH¢10,000+ sustainably harvested. Why It Matters: Year-round income, erosion control, community development, and global exports.

MODULE VII — Fire Patrol: The Forest's Greatest Enemy

Bushfires destroy more forest than axes. A ranger's daily fight: Clearing firebreaks, patrolling Harmattan seasons, educating farmers on controlled burning, rapid response with water packs, tools, and drones.

One spark = thousands of cedis lost. One watchman = forests

saved.

Quick Fact: Harmattan (Nov–Feb) causes 80% of Ghana's forest fires.

Reflection Prompt: Which task excites you most: fighting fires, planting trees, or studying wildlife? Why?

MODULE VIII — Modern Tools & Training Pathways

Technology meets tradition: GPS mapping, drone-spotting illegal logging, apps tracking tree growth, drip-irrigated nurseries, and solar-powered ranger stations.

Pathways in Ghana: SHS Agriculture + TVET Forestry, MOFA Forestry apprenticeships, KNUST Forestry degrees, Forestry Commission cadet programs.

Career Levels: 1. Forest Guard patrols, planting, basic surveying. 2. Forest Ranger supervises, manages nurseries, and leads fire response. 3. Professional Forester designs plans, research, and oversees zones.

Focus on Biology, Geography, Math, and ICT. Join wildlife clubs, Scouts, and climate action teams.

MODULE IX — Business Sense In Forestry

A forester thinks like an entrepreneur: Calculate timber volume, time harvests for peak price, package shea butter for export, and train communities for eco-tourism.

Youth grants fund: 1-hectare woodlots, 500-tree nurseries, and honey processing units. Small starts → sustainable wealth.

Reflection Prompt: Which forest product could you turn into a business for your community?

MODULE X — The Personal Side of Forestry

Forestry demands grit: early patrols, long days in the heat, nights guarding against poachers, and constant learning. But rewards heal the soul: first, seedlings sprouting; first, a sustainable harvest; birds returning; knowing your work fights climate change.

Forestry offers purpose, stability, and national service.

MODULE XI — Is This Your Path?

Ask yourself: Do trees calm your spirit? Can you spot dying branches from healthy ones? Do you love math when measuring trees? Does protecting nature feel like a purpose? Would you enjoy weeks in remote forests?

If yes, you're not failing academics, you're called to heal the earth.

FINAL WORD — Hands That Plant Futures

Forestry isn't fallback work. It is: Intelligence measuring sustainable yields, discipline patrolling through storms, vision seeing 50-year tree growth, stewardship protecting creation, courage facing fire and poachers.

Your boots mark trails. Your hands plant futures.

Work with trees, and you will: Shade generations, fight climate change, restore degraded lands, build nations that breathe easy, guard rivers, wildlife, tomorrow.

You're not "just planting trees." You're securing life itself.

07

HAIR & BEAUTY

*Blameless Architects of Appearance,
Hairdressers, Barbers & Makeup Masters
Who Polish Humanity's Dignity*

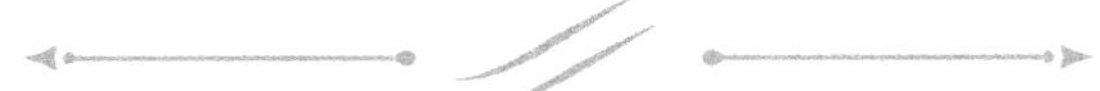

MODULE I — The Eternal Weight of Polished Appearance

BEFORE SURGEONS HEALED BODIES, BARBERS restored dignity; before psychologists named trauma, hairdressers heard it, your chair, their confessional. Before presidents addressed nations, makeup artists prepared their faces for the world.

A haircut restores dignity. Makeup unveils inner strength. A styled look transforms lives.

Beauty work began around ancient fires, elders adorning warriors for battle, brides for unions, mourners for healing.

From that dawn, hairdressers, barbers, and makeup artists became sacred custodians of human confidence and eternal transformation.

This vocation rivals medicine: Doctors heal bodies. Beauty artisans heal self-worth. Presidents command podiums with your polish. News anchors deliver truth through your composure. Wedding couples vow eternity under your artistry. Every mirror reflects your hand. They hear secrets presidents never hear, witness transformations doctors never see, build trust pastors cannot always reach.

Generation Alpha, your scissors hold power: Polish presidents or peddle illusions? Style for service, not selfies. Glamour harvests likes. Transformation harvests destinies. A nation's confidence begins in its mirrors.

MODULE II — When Society Turns To Its Polishers

In transitions, weddings forging families, elections shaping nations, broadcasts uniting millions, funerals honoring legacies, society seeks masters. Your chair becomes a sanctuary, canvas for courage. From Accra to Lagos, Mississippi to Mumbai, barbershops and salons are confessional havens.

Beauty artisans shape: Presidents poised for world stages, News casters framing national truth, Wedding couples radiating eternal vows, Job seekers unlocking doors with first impressions, Grieving families finding dignified solace, Youth performers silencing doubters with shine.

Clients enter anxious, insecure, grieving, hopeful, for interviews, heartbreak healing, transformation. They leave renewed, confident, ready. Beauty professionals become counselors, mentors, protectors, cultural ambassadors, emotional stabilizers.

A good barber can stop a young man from joining a gang. A hairdresser can restore a woman's confidence after trauma. Beauty is prophecy: Careless hands wound self-image. Blameless ones elevate souls. This is nation-building.

MODULE III — The Artisan's Sacred Duties

Beyond salons lies guardianship. The beauty master's mandate:

1. **Dignity Restoration** — Transforming insecurity into unshakeable poise.
2. **Cultural Preservation** — Weaving Adinkra braids, fades honoring Ashanti kings.
3. **Confidence Amplification** — Polishing presidents while humbling egos.
4. **Ethical Stewardship** — Rejecting harmful chemicals, toxic trends.
5. **Youth Mentorship** — Training apprentices who outshine masters.
6. **Institutional Legacy** — Building salon empires training thousands.
7. **Crisis Response** — Free styling for disaster victims, hospital glow-ups.
8. **Global–Local Bridge** — Exporting Ghanaian braiding beyond Africa.

They restore confidence, preserve culture, create jobs, support mental health, drive economies (GH¢562M beauty sector by 2027, 12% CAGR). Success measures in transformed lives, unbreakable confidence, generational wealth.

MODULE III-A — Braiding Masters: Weaving Identity & Culture

Braiding is storytelling, heritage, confidence spun into strands. From Accra markets to global runways, braiders shape identities and empower communities.

Each braid carries history: cornrows, box braids, Ghana braids, Fulani braids, twists, updos, bridal styles connecting generations. Cultural Guardianship. Ghanaian traditions honor ancestors, signal status, celebrate milestones. Confidence Crafting. A child's first cornrows, bride's wedding braid, performer's stage style transforms self-esteem. Economic Architecture. Market stalls, mobile services, salons, online tutorials (20% salons employ 50K+ by 2026). Mentorship & Mastery. Apprenticeship demands precision, patience, hygiene, empathy. Global Reach. From Ghana to Hollywood, exporting culture and style.

A braider listens before weaving, fear, excitement, joy, grief flow into every strand. Careless hands fracture confidence. Blameless hands weave pride into generations.

MODULE IV — Madam C.J. Walker: Orphan to Haircare Empress

Sarah Breedlove picked cotton on Delta plantations, orphaned at 7, widowed at 20, laundry worker in Denver. At 38, her vegetable-oil tonic restored her hair and birthed an empire: Age 41: Opened Pittsburgh salon, trained 1,000 stylists. Age 44: Built factories, five salons across America. Age 51: Died as America's first self-made female millionaire ($600K, $8M today).

She funded Black colleges, YMCA, NAACP anti-lynching campaigns. Temperament of steel: She listened to women's sorrows before building their wealth ladders. Hairdressers do not style locks. They build empires.

MODULE IV-B — Akosua Boateng: Accra Braider to Global Exporter

From Makola market stalls, Akosua Boateng launched a $500K shea-hair product line by 2023, training 200 apprentices. Her Ghana braids graced London Fashion Week, blending Adinkra heritage with modern shine. Rising from street braids, she proves: Local hands fuel global dynasties.

MODULE V — Vernon Winfrey: Billionaire's Barber, Deacon of Service

Vernon Winfrey rose from Mississippi dirt floors, Korean War trenches, Vanderbilt pot-scrubbing: Age 31 (1964): Opened Winfrey Barber & Beauty Shop. Age 42 (1975): Elected councilman while cutting hair. Age 79 (2012): Oprah repurchased his shop, he kept working. Age 89 (2022): Honored with "Vernon Winfrey Day."

He cut hair 50+ years, rejecting billionaire luxury for service. Lesson: Billionaire fathers fade. Service cuts eternal.

MODULE VI — Makeup Masters: Face Painters of Power

Makeup artists prepare faces for boardrooms, ballots, broadcasts, weddings, global premieres. They blend chemistry with empathy, concealing scars, revealing strength.

One brush stroke moves a million minds. Makeup manifests identity, sculpts confidence, softens anxiety. It is emotional restoration.

MODULE VII — God-Given Hands, Polished To Precision

DIVINE SPARK	DISCIPLINED FORGE	LEGACY EMPIRE
Touch (Walker)	Cotton-to-salon toil	40K women trained
Scissors (Vernon)	War pots to council	Oprah saved, communities healed
Brush (Makeup)	Client confessions	Presidents poised, nations swayed
Braids (Boateng)	Market stalls to runways	200 apprentices, $500K exports

God gifts hands. Discipline builds dynasties.

MODULE VIII — SHS Foundations & Paths to Beauty Mastery

SHS Bedrock

SUBJECT	BEAUTY FORGE	ETERNAL CRAFT
Science	Chemistry/ Biology	Safe tonics, scalp health
Art	Design/Color Theory	Fades, bridal visions
English	Consultation	Confidence dialogue
Home Science	Hygiene/ Nutrition	Healthy hair from root
ICT	Booking/Trends	Global branding

Skills Table

FOUNDATION	SHS SUBJECT	SKILL DEVELOPED
Precision	Mathematics	Cutting angles, symmetry
Creativity	Visual Arts	Style design, makeup blending
Communication	English	Confidence dialogue, branding
Hygiene	Integrated Science	Scalp/skin care
Entrepreneurship	Business	Salon chains, exports
Cultural Depth	History/Social	Adinkra braids, Ashanti fades

Diverse Paths to Wealth: Apprenticeship → Master → Chain (e.g., 20% Ghana salons employ 50K+ by 2026). SHS Visual Arts → Beauty College → International competitions. Street braids → Product line → Factory → Global export ($46M skin care market). Barber → Councilman → Policy for 1M stylists.

Training Path:

1. SHS Foundation
2. Apprenticeship (1–3 years)
3. Certification
4. Professional Practice
5. Entrepreneurship

Beauty work is scalable, global, profitable ($59.5M skin care by 2026).

MODULE IX — Perils: Scissors That Wound Instead Of Heal

Mirrors lie: Toxic chemicals, Copycat styles, Overpricing, Trend-chasing. One bad cut ripples shame eternally. One masterful touch restores generations.

MODULE X — Legacy: From Salon Chair To National Thrones

Politicians chase votes. Beauty masters chase confidence. Amid Galamsey scars, your brushes heal widows, steady election anchors, fueling 20M faces in a $562M sector.

Ask: Does this style unlock doors a decade from now? Does this training birth stylists who outshine me? Does this product empower thousands?

MODULE XI — Oath Of The Blameless Beauty Artisan

"I polish appearances that unveil inner strength. I cut confidence into every crown. I blend faces framing truth for nations. I train hands that outlive my own. I reject vanity's poison for dignity's cure. I build salon empires serving generations. I leave every client richer in spirit than skin.

I shape identity with dignity. I honor my craft with discipline. I treat every client with respect. I build wealth through service. I uplift my community with my hands. I leave every face and head better than I found it."

FINAL DECREE

Walker rose from cotton to empress. Vernon rejected billions for brotherhood. Boateng wove Makola into runways. Makeup masters anoint presidents.

Your SHS hands cradle tomorrow's thrones. Galamsey widows need your bridal glow. Election anchors demand your brushes.

20M Ghanaian faces watch: Style, or transform? Ugly insecurity dies when blameless artisans multiply.

Rise, humanity's eternal polishers. Confidence breathes your craft. Beauty work is nation-shaping, identity-building, wealth-creating.

KITCHEN &
FLAVOR EMPIRE

MODULE I — Three Flavors That Feed Nations

IMAGINE THIS. OSU, ACCRA, AT SEVEN IN THE MORNING. A quiet kitchen releases the scent of passion fruit into the street. A former banker, hands still trembling from the decision she made the day before, watches a commuter pause, taste her creation, and whisper, "This is Ghana." Her new life begins with that single bite.

Imagine this. Suame trotro stop in Kumasi. By mid-morning, Kojo has served his four-hundred-and-fiftieth plate of waakye. Rice, beans, eggs, shito, gari consistent, comforting, reliable. Truck drivers park their vehicles and say, "This fuel keeps Ghana moving." Six months earlier, he started with GH₵650 and a borrowed table.

Imagine this. A food court in East Legon. Efua, an SHS Home Economics graduate, faces her first queue of executives. Her grandmother's spice blend simmers in every pot. Her sign reads, "Taste Ghana's soul." She is saving for her first food truck.

These scenes reveal a simple truth: food is not merely fuel. It is culture, comfort, and community. And for SHS and JHS graduates, your recipes can feed nations.

MODULE II — The Passion Fruit Pioneer

In 2013, a young professional in Osu left a stable banking job salary, structure, security because one idea refused to leave her mind. Every evening, her small kitchen became a laboratory. Passion-fruit curd bright as Ghanaian sunshine. Chocolate ganache perfected through patience. Mango cheesecake celebrating local abundance.

Day one: she walked the streets of Osu offering samples to strangers. Week three: her first wedding order. Month six: corporate deliveries. Year two: supermarket shelves.

Today, her brand stands as a decade-strong presence in Accra, training young bakers from Osu, Madina, and Tema, and supplying major retailers. Industry benchmarks place her monthly revenue above GH¢11,000.

One flavor obsession, disciplined daily, became a national enterprise.

MODULE III — Silvia Paulino: Heritage To Empire

In 2002, Silvia arrived in Philadelphia from the Dominican Republic. She spoke little English. She had no savings. But she carried her grandmother's recipes on folded paper.

Tres leches that tasted like home. Empanadas crisp with memory. Guava pastries sweet with nostalgia. Month one: she baked in her home kitchen and knocked on neighbors' doors. Year two: neighborhood children called her "Tia Silvia." Year five: community events became her stage. By 2019: she opened a 1,500-square-foot bakery with local staff and an SBA loan.

Today, families celebrate birthdays at her shop. Teenagers learn their first job skills behind her counter. Her bakery is a community anchor.

Heritage, when managed with discipline, becomes an empire.

MODULE IV — Enga Stanfield: From Failure To A GH¢70 Million Chain

In Texas, Mattenga's Pizzeria was collapsing empty tables, frustrated staff, annual losses in the millions. Most people would have closed the doors. Enga Stanfield did not.

She rebuilt the business through discipline and systems: early-morning training videos, AI-supported scheduling, community giveaways, and consistent quality. The turnaround was steady and remarkable.

Year one: break even. Year three: profitability. Year five: a multi-location chain valued at more than GH¢70 million. Year seven: national awards and recognition.

She proved that recipes do not build empires systems and community do.

MODULE V — The Housekeeping Principle

Running a restaurant or bakery is housekeeping on a large scale. What a parent does for five people, a restaurant manager does for fifty, five hundred, or five thousand.

Meals planned. Ingredients purchased. Spaces cleaned. People welcomed. Budgets balanced.

Cooking is ten percent of the work. Management is ninety.

MODULE VI — Ghana's Food Goldmine

Ghana's food economy is expanding rapidly. Waakye stalls serve millions of plates daily. Jollof anchors weddings and celebrations. Desserts attract urban youth. Catering powers schools, offices, and events.

Opportunities exist in bakeries, cafeterias, catering companies, food trucks, tea rooms, and small restaurants. Ghana needs cooks, managers, supervisors, baristas, pastry chefs, food safety officers, and entrepreneurs.

MODULE VII — Skills And Subjects

SKILL	SUBJECT	APPLICATION
Measurement	Mathematics	Scaling recipes, costing
Nutrition	Science	Food safety, shelf life
Accounting	Business	Pricing, budgeting
Communication	English	Customer relations
Technology	CT	POS systems, delivery apps
Design	Creative Arts	Presentation, branding

School subjects become the backbone of a food empire.

MODULE VIII — Startup Kitchen (GH₵3,800)

A basic startup kitchen requires approximately GH₵3,800: A gas oven, mixers, whisks, pots, pans, and a small display case. A commercial kitchen upgrade ranges around GH₵28,000.

Small beginnings can grow into national brands.

MODULE IX — The Ten Laws Of Food Empires

1. Cleanliness protects your license.
2. Consistency builds trust.
3. Service shapes memory.
4. Training strengthens teams.
5. Waste destroys profit.
6. Systems scale; talent alone does not.
7. Community creates loyalty.
8. Branding earns premium pricing.
9. Quality builds reputation.
10. Innovation sustains longevity.

MODULE X — JHS To Flavor Empire

LEVEL	TIME	ROLE	INCOME
1	6–12 months	Kitchen helper	GH₵650–1,800
2	1–3 years	Stall owner	GH₵3,200–7,500
3	3–5 years	Supervisor	GH₵9,000–16,000
4	5+ years	Chain owner	GH₵35,000+

Growth follows discipline, not degrees.

FINAL WORD — Your Oven Awaits

The passion-fruit pioneer built a dessert culture from a home kitchen. Silvia turned heritage into a community institution. Enga transformed a failing pizzeria into a multimillion-cedi chain. Kojo grew GH¢650 into hundreds of daily plates.

Two paths stand before you: Office work: GH¢1,500 and monthly reports. Kitchen work: GH¢35,000+ and millions served.

Ghana needs innovators of flavor waakye masters, jollof specialists, pastry pioneers, and culinary visionaries.

Generation Alpha, the world is hungry for your ideas. What flavor empire will you build first.

MAKER EMPIRE: THE MANUFACTURERS WHO BUILD NATIONS

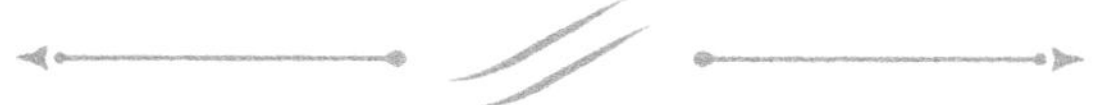

MODULE I — The Forge Of Human Progress

(An Allegory for Generation Alpha)

IMAGINE THIS. A FACTORY FLOOR IN ACCRA, SHENZHEN, Detroit, or Nairobi. Machines hum. Sparks fly. Conveyor belts glide past. A young apprentice stands at a workstation, holding a simple tool.

A supervisor walks past and says: "Everything you see   every phone, every shoe, every car, every book   began in the hands of someone like you."

Imagine this. A textile mill in Kumasi. A young woman threads a loom, turning cotton into fabric that will clothe thousands in Ghana, Europe, and America.

Imagine this. A metal workshop in Takoradi. A teenager welds steel that will become part of a bridge, a ship, a school desk.

Imagine this. A robotics lab in Tema. A young engineer programs a machine that will assemble solar panels for villages across Africa.

These scenes are not history. They are possibility. They are allegory. They are the future Generation Alpha can build anywhere in the world.

One truth remains: Manufacturing is the backbone of every modern nation. SHS/JHS graduates your hands can build the world.

MODULE II — Greta Thunberg: When One Teen Shifts Global Industry

2018, Sweden. A shy 15-year-old schoolgirl sits alone outside parliament with a cardboard sign: "School Strike for Climate."

No wealth. No connections. No authority. Just conviction. Within a year, that solitary strike grows into Fridays for Future millions of students across continents demanding climate action.

Governments respond. Companies rewrite sustainability targets. Manufacturing giants rethink: emissions, materials, energy use, waste reduction.

Greta does not own a factory. But she influences factories.

Lesson for Generation Alpha: You may not own industry yet but you can influence how industry behaves.

MODULE III — What Manufacturing Really Is

Manufacturing comes from manus (hand) and facio (make). Today it means: Turning raw materials into products that make life possible.

Wood → desks, doors, furniture

Cotton → uniforms, Kente, garments

Iron ore → steel → bridges

Sand → glass → windows, screens

Cocoa → chocolate, cosmetics

Look around you. Everything you see was designed, refined, and manufactured.

Manufacturing is not noise. It is civilization in motion.

MODULE IV — From Handcraft To Smart Factories

Generations ago: Soap made by hand. Clothes sewn at home. Furniture built locally.

Then came: Steam power. Assembly lines. Electric motors. Industrial robots. 3D printing. AI-guided systems.

Machines multiply effort. But machines still need: Designers - Technicians - Operators - Entrepreneurs.

Machines multiply effort. Humans multiply meaning.

MODULE V — Why Manufacturing Builds Nations

Strong economies build things. Manufacturing: creates jobs, adds value, reduces imports, drives innovation, builds resilience.

Nations that produce lead. Nations that import everything depend.

Africa's next leap will come from: processing - assembling - manufacturing. Not exporting raw materials alone.

MODULE VI — Why Africa Must Manufacture

Africa holds: the cocoa - the gold - the bauxite - the timber - the oil - the lithium - the sunlight - the workforce.

Yet much of the value is captured elsewhere. Manufacturing is how Africa: keeps wealth at home, stops exporting opportunity, rises.

MODULE VII — Ghana's Manufacturing Goldmines

Opportunities include: Textiles & garments, Food processing, Furniture, Automotive assembly, Plastics & packaging, Pharmaceuticals, Metal fabrication, Renewable energy components.

Across Tema, Kumasi, Takoradi, Tamale, and Accra, workshops and factories need: Welders - Machine operators - Designers - Technicians - Engineers - Quality inspectors - Entrepreneurs.

Ghana can be a maker nation.

MODULE VIII — Makers Who Changed The World

Henry Ford The Assembly Line Architect. He redesigned how cars were built. Production sped up. Prices dropped. Industry changed.

Soichiro Honda From Scrap to Global Brand. He began with bicycle engines built from leftovers. He built motorcycles. Then cars. Then a global company.

Madam C.J. Walker From Kitchen to Factory. She solved a problem. Built a product. Built factories. Built wealth.

Taiichi Ohno The Worker Who Reinvented Production. Post-war Japan. Toyota was struggling. Waste was everywhere.

Taiichi Ohno was not a CEO. He was a factory worker. He observed inefficiency. Eliminated waste. Created the Toyota Production System: produce only what is needed, eliminate excess inventory, empower workers to stop errors, improve continuously.

This became Lean Manufacturing. One worker reshaped global industry.

MODULE VIII-B — Akosua Afrifa: The Ghanaian Who Turned Plastic Into Power

1998, Kumasi. Akosua Afrifa graduates with a chemistry degree and notices something everyone else ignores: Ghana imports almost every plastic bottle it uses.

Water bottlers import PET preforms. Pharmacies import pill bottles. Cosmetic companies import containers. Food processors import packaging. Millions of cedis leave Ghana every month.

Akosua asks: "Why can't we make these here?" She rents a small warehouse in Kaase. Buys a single second-hand injection-molding machine. Sleeps on a mattress beside the machine for the first six months.

Her first products: PET preforms - Bottle caps - Small cosmetic jars - Pharmaceutical containers. She walks from shop to shop with samples in a backpack.

First clients: sachet water companies - local pharmacies - shea butter cooperatives - small beverage startups. Demand grows. She reinvests every cedi.

By 2010: 12 injection-molding machines - 4 blow-molding lines - recycling unit. By 2020: Supplies Coca-Cola, Voltic, Unilever.

Factory runs 24 hours. 450 workers employed. Exports to Togo, Côte d'Ivoire, Liberia, Sierra Leone.

2026: Afrifa Plastics = West Africa's #1 PET bottle maker. Supplies: Coca-Cola, Voltic, Unilever, pharmacies. Exports: Togo, Côte d'Ivoire, Liberia. Jobs: 450 workers trained. Impact: Cuts Ghana's plastic import bill by millions monthly.

Truth: Akosua did not wait for permission. She saw a gap. She built a factory. She changed an industry.

Lesson: Local problems are global opportunities in disguise.

MODULE IX — Allegories Of Ghana's Makers

Kofi — welding apprentice to workshop owner

Efua — assembly worker to solar systems leader

Kwame — garment helper to export factory founder

Starting small is not shameful. Staying small in vision is.

MODULE X — The Maker's Toolbox

SKILL	SUBJECT	FACTORY USE
Precision	Mathematics	Measurement/ costing
Design	Technical Drawing	Blueprints
Materials	Chemistry	Plastics/metals
Motion	Physics	Machines
Systems	ICT	Automation

School is preparation for production.

MODULE XI — The Maker Mindset

To build, you need: Curiosity - Patience - Precision - Problem-solving - Resilience - Discipline - Imagination.

Tools matter. Machines matter. But mindset is the true engine of manufacturing.

MODULE XII — The Factory Of The Future

Tomorrow's factories will use: Robotics - AI systems - Sensors - Renewable energy - Digital simulation.

Generation Alpha will: work in them - run them - own them - redesign them.

MODULE XIII — Pathways Into Manufacturing

Apprentice

Technician

Designer

Engineer

Quality inspector

Entrepreneur

Certificates open doors. Skill keeps you inside.

MODULE XIV — The Ten Laws Of Makers

1. Measure carefully.
2. Protect quality.
3. Guard safety.
4. Respect time.
5. Learn continuously.
6. Understand costs.

7. Improve systems.
8. Document processes.
9. Collaborate wisely.
10. Think generationally.

MODULE XV — Seasons Of Opportunity

School openings

Harvest seasons

Festivals

Election periods

Manufacturers who study timing grow.

FINAL WORD — Build

Factories are where ideas become objects. Where imagination becomes industry. Where hands turn raw earth into global value.

The machines are ready. The workshops are ready. The markets are ready. Not for someone else. For you.

The world is waiting for its next maker. Would you answer the call?

10

MINNING

*Legal Mining, Galamsey, and the Future
of Ghana's Land*

*For Generation Alpha in Ghana
and Across the World*

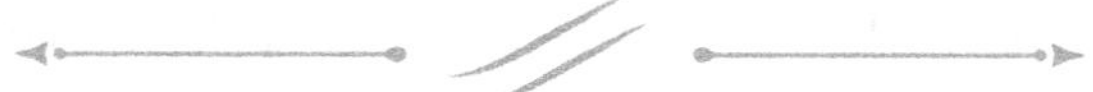

MODULE I — Two Things That Look Alike But Are Not The Same

THERE ARE MANY THINGS IN THIS WORLD WHICH are very much alike, and yet are totally dissimilar. Two rivers may begin from the same hill, yet one gives life and the other spreads disease. Two fires may glow with the same flame, yet one cooks food and the other burns homes.

Mining in Ghana is like this. From a distance, legal mining and Galamsey appear similar. Both dig. Both search for gold. Both touch the same earth. But what they produce and what they destroy are entirely different.

One is patient. The other is desperate. One builds quietly. The other consumes loudly. They use the same ground, yet they leave behind opposite futures.

MODULE II — What Legal Mining Really Is

Legal mining is not speed. It is discipline. It begins with study of rock, water, pressure, and balance. Before the land is touched, the mind has already worked.

Legal mining asks: Where will the water flow? How will the ground be supported? How will workers be protected? What will the land look like after we leave?

It is slow by design. Careful by necessity. Legal mining understands one truth: the earth is powerful, and power demands respect.

MODULE III — What Galamsey Really Is

Galamsey is not small mining. It is not informal mining. It is not "people trying to survive." Galamsey is extraction without knowledge. Speed without planning. Taking without responsibility.

It does not ask what happens after. It only asks what can be taken now. Rivers are treated as tools. Forests are treated as obstacles. Children are treated as labor.

Galamsey does not listen to the land. It forces it. And the land always responds.

MODULE IV — The Land Remembers The Difference

Legal mining leaves marks that can heal. Galamsey leaves wounds that remain. Where legal mining ends, land is reshaped, soil restored, trees replanted. Where Galamsey passes, the earth collapses inward pits filled with poison, water turned thick and lifeless.

A forest cut for impatience does not return quickly. A river poisoned by carelessness does not forget. The land keeps memory longer than people do.

MODULE V — Rivers That Once Fed Communities

There were rivers in Ghana that once ran clear enough for children to see their feet. They fed farms. They carried fish. They held stories. When Galamsey entered them, the water changed color—not once, but permanently.

Communities downstream stopped drinking. Farmers stopped irrigating. Fish disappeared. A dead river does not announce its death. It simply stops giving.

Stand by a river at dawn and watch the water move. You will understand what Ghana loses each time Galamsey wins.

MODULE VI — Farms That Can No Longer Grow

Gold does not feed a nation. Soil does. When fertile land is stripped and soaked in chemicals, farming does not return easily. Roots fail. Crops weaken. Fields are abandoned.

Legal mining protects surrounding farms because it understands interdependence. Galamsey destroys them because it does not look beyond today. A nation that poisons its farms borrows hunger from the future.

MODULE VII — Forests And The Balance They Hold

Forests are not decoration. They are systems. They guide rain. They cool the land. They hold soil in place. They protect rivers. When forests are cleared recklessly, the balance breaks.

Heat increases. Floods worsen. Dry seasons stretch longer. Legal mining plans around forests. Galamsey removes them without memory. Nature does not punish. It responds.

MODULE VIII — The Poison That Travels

Some damage stays where it begins. Other damage moves. Mercury does not remain in one pit. It enters water. It enters fish. It enters food. Children who never stepped near a mine feel its effects years later.

This is the quiet cruelty of Galamsey: those who gain little are harmed the most.

MODULE IX — Childhoods Taken Underground

Justice Afekey was once just a schoolboy. When Galamsey pulled him underground, it did not only take his education. It took time—years that do not return. Darkness became normal. Danger became routine. Poison became air.

He did not emerge rich. He emerged changed. Galamsey does not create success stories. It creates survivors. And Justice is not alone.

Three brothers Sampson, Elshaddai, and Yaw were lured with promises of gold and school fees. Instead, they met mercury exposure, beatings, starvation, and child slavery. They escaped at night, guided by fear and hope.

When a child enters Galamsey, a future dies.

MODULE X — The Economic Lie

Galamsey promises fast money. It rarely delivers lasting value. Gold leaves the country. Communities remain poor. Land becomes useless.

Legal mining, when done well, trains people, builds skills, and supports public life long after extraction ends. Shortcuts enrich a few. Systems build nations.

MODULE XI — Safety Is A Moral Choice

In legal mining, safety is planned before profit. Tunnels are reinforced. Air is monitored. Rescue teams stand ready. In Galamsey, safety is hope.

Cave-ins are expected. Deaths go unrecorded. Children work where adults hesitate. How a society protects its workers reveals how it values life.

MODULE XII — Technology As Restraint

Modern mining uses technology not to dominate the earth, but to understand it. Mapping tools see before digging. Sensors warn before collapse. Systems reduce waste and restore balance.

Technology does not replace judgment. It strengthens it. Galamsey rejects knowledge because knowledge slows it down.

MODULE XIII — Ghana's Name Beyond Its Borders

What happens to land here is felt elsewhere. Gold carries reputation. Rivers carry consequences. Environmental neglect travels farther than borders.

The world watches how Ghana treats its ground not because it is curious, but because it is connected.

MODULE XIV — The Paths That Were Always There

Justice Afekey's life could have followed another road. Science classrooms. Careful training. Work done in daylight. Legal mining offers careers that protect life rather than gamble with it.

The tragedy is not that options do not exist. It is that shortcuts hide them.

MODULE XV — A Question For Generation Alpha

Two paths still lie before Ghana. One looks fast. The other looks slow. One takes. The other builds. They may appear similar at first glance. But only one leaves land that can still breathe.

FINAL WORD — What Will Still Stand

Mining is not judged by what is removed from the ground. It is judged by what remains afterward. Rivers that still flow. Land that still grows. Communities that still live.

Generation Alpha, the earth will answer how you treat it. Choose knowledge over haste. Stewardship over hunger. Life over poison. Two things may look alike. But the land always knows the difference.

11

POULTRY, LIVESTOCK & DAIRY

MODULE I — When Books Feel Heavy But Living Things Make Sense

SOME YOUNG PEOPLE UNDERSTAND THE WORLD through pages. Others understand it through patterns. Kwame was the second kind. He tried in school. He memorized notes. He attended extra classes. He prayed before every exam. Still, numbers slipped, paragraphs blurred, and essays felt like fog.

One Saturday morning, while helping his mother feed their chickens, he noticed something: He could tell which hen was stressed. Which one was about to lay. Which one was sick? Which one was bullying the others?

He didn't learn this from a book. He learned it from watching.

His mother whispered, "Some people read words. Some people read life."

That thought settled inside him like a quiet truth.

Fun Fact for Gen Alpha: Hens can remember up to 100 different faces—including humans! Observing them carefully teaches awareness and patience.

MODULE II — Practical Intelligence In Action

A neighbor's goat refused to eat. Suggestions flew: salt, herbs, guesses. Kwame crouched beside the animal, checked its gums, observed its breathing, and said: "It's not eating because it's in pain. Something is stuck."

He carefully opened its mouth, removed a thorn, and watched the goat chew again.

The neighbor stared. "How did you know?"

Kwame shrugged. "I just watched."

That evening, he realized, "Maybe my mind is not slow. Maybe it is built for living things."

Reflection Prompt: Think of a time you noticed something no one else did. How could observing closely help you solve bigger problems?

MODULE III — Northern Nigeria Dairy Farmers

In northern Nigeria, many young dairy farmers have built thriving businesses from almost nothing, just a few cows on small plots of land. They started during difficult economic times: Feed was expensive. Veterinary care was scarce. Dry seasons were harsh. But they stayed determined.

These farmers learned modern techniques from local co-ops: Improved feeding, basic veterinary care, clean milking practices, and simple record-keeping. They sold fresh milk to neighbors, reinvesting every profit to buy more animals. Some seasons brought disease or drought. But they kept going.

Today, many have grown from a handful of cows to large herds that supply milk across regions, employ local youth, use innovations like solar pumps, and share their journeys on Facebook farming groups as models of grit and progress.

For Generation Alpha in Ghana and beyond, these true stories show: You don't need perfect conditions. You need consistency, curiosity, and courage.

Did You Know? A single dairy cow can provide up to 20 liters of milk a day under proper care, enough to feed 10–15 children every day.

Reflection Prompt: If you had a small plot and one cow, how would you start? What would your first step be?

MODULE IV — Animals As A Classroom

Working with animals is not "village work." It is science, business, and service combined.

Livestock, dairy, and poultry farming require Observation and patience, pattern recognition and decision-making, hygiene, nutrition, and disease control, breeding science and record-keeping, business sense, and marketing.

This is applied science with a heartbeat.

MODULE V — Poultry: Small Creatures, Big Impact

Chickens, ducks, guinea fowls, and turkeys look simple, but poultry farming is highly technical.

A skilled farmer manages: Temperature and humidity, feed formulation, lighting schedules, vaccination programs, stocking density, and biosecurity.

Even a single mistake, such as overcrowding, dirty water, or wrong feed, can wipe out a flock. But a single correct decision, clean bedding, balanced feed, and proper ventilation can double production.

Why Poultry Matters: Eggs provide daily protein to families, schools, and hospitals. Meat supports hotels, restaurants, and markets. Automated incubators, drinkers, and climate-controlled sheds maximize yield. Export markets are growing steadily.

Starting small, a young farmer can grow a backyard flock into a full-fledged business.

Fun Fact: Chickens can lay one egg almost every day for months, making them a consistent source of nutrition and income.

MODULE VI — Livestock: Understanding Larger Lives

Livestock farming includes goats, sheep, cattle, pigs, and rabbits.

Each animal speaks its own language: Goats communicate stress with bleats, sheep show illness through movement, pigs reveal discomfort through appetite, and cattle express health through posture.

A good farmer reads these signs like a book.

Tasks include: Balancing feed for growth and health,

monitoring breeding cycles, preventing parasites, maintaining hygiene, managing grazing and pastures, planning markets and seasonal sales.

Why Livestock Matters: Meat demand is rising locally and globally; goats and sheep are major exports; pig farming is growing rapidly, offering high-protein meat; livestock manure enriches soils for crops; and farmers contribute to food security and nutrition.

Reflection Prompt: Can you notice small signs of change around you, like Kwame with his animals? How could that skill help you in school or life?

MODULE VII — Dairy: Daily Discipline, Daily Nutrition

Dairy farming is one of the most disciplined vocations. Cows and goats do not wait. They must be milked on time every day.

A dairy farmer must understand: Animal comfort and nutrition, milking hygiene and milk storage, disease prevention, breeding cycles, and record-keeping.

Why Dairy Matters: Milk, yogurt, cheese, and butter are daily essentials. Schools and hospitals depend on dairy for nutrition. Urban markets demand a consistent supply. Farmers earn a steady income and build respected businesses.

Quick Fact: Holsteins produce high-volume milk, Jerseys produce rich milk, and local breeds are hardy with lower maintenance.

MODULE VIII — Modern Farming Tools & Techniques

Modern animal farming blends tradition with technology: Feed mixers, tractors, and automatic waterers, solar-powered poultry ventilation and dairy chillers, veterinary care and nutritional programs, record-keeping software and market research, diversification: poultry + goats, dairy + fodder crops = risk management.

Education matters. SHS agriculture, TVET, NVTI, and agricultural colleges give an edge. Apprenticeships and online resources supplement learning.

MODULE IX — Business Sense In Farming

A farmer is a scientist and a salesperson. Eggs and milk must be packaged cleanly. Goats and sheep must meet weight standards. Customers return when trust and service are consistent. Youth loans from NBSSI or microfinance can help start small flocks or dairy units.

Even a small starter like 200 layers or a few goats can grow into profitable businesses with discipline and smart management.

MODULE X — The Personal Side Of Farming

Animal farming is not easy: Early mornings and long hours, consistency and patience, physical work and outdoor exposure, emotional resilience for sickness or losses, and continuous learning.

But rewards are real: The first egg laid, the first kid born, the first liter of milk sold, feeding families, schools, and communities, gaining independence, skill, and respect.

MODULE XI — Is This Your Path?

Ask yourself: Do animals calm you? Do you notice small changes in behavior? Do you enjoy practical work? Do you feel responsible when caring for living things?

If yes, you are not "falling back." You are aligning with your strength, intelligence, and purpose.

FINAL WORD — Caring For Lives That Feed Lives

Poultry, livestock, and dairy farming are life-sustaining vocations.

They require: Intelligence, discipline, compassion, science, courage.

Your hands are instruments. Your mind is the tool.

Work with living things, and you will feed communities, strengthen nations, and protect futures.

12

RETAILER

The Young Person Who Wanted to Become a Retail Strategist

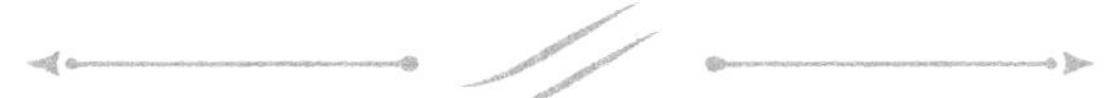

MODULE I — The Invitation: A Young Mind At The Market Edge

IT IS A BRIGHT AFTERNOON IN ACCRA. AT THE EDGE of a busy market stall, a young person sits quietly, watching the world move at full speed. Delivery bikes weave through traffic. WhatsApp orders ping. Instagram Reels flash trends. Everyone is loud, rushing, and distracted. No one notices the quiet thinker at the corner.

They are not chasing attention.
Not following noise.
They are thinking.

They imagine a modern store not theirs yet, not famous, but alive with purpose. Products are arranged so customers can easily find what they need. Sneakers sourced from Turkey, chargers from Shenzhen, cocoa from Côte d'Ivoire. Displays designed to make customers pause, smile, and choose. Systems are organized, while others rush into confusion.

They whisper, "I want to be a retail strategist."

Adults smile politely. Some laugh. Some dismiss it as "shop work."

But purpose hides where the world is too busy to look.

This path is not small. Not "less than." Not a fallback.

In Ghana, Africa, and across the world, retail strategy is strategic, creative, analytical, and upward-moving.

MODULE II — Breakfast, Hoodies, And The Global Story

Every morning, your breakfast tells a global story:

ITEM	ORIGIN
Oranges	California
Oats	Kansas
Eggs	Volta Region
Cocoa	Brazil / Tema
Muffins	Pennsylvania

Your hoodie? Cotton from Egypt, dyed in Ghana, stitched in Vietnam.

Your sneakers? Leather from Italy, soles from China, assembled in Ethiopia.

Every item traveled across continents, through warehouses, and through digital systems before reaching you.

Who Made This Possible?

Retail strategists:
Compared supplier prices
Checked factory quality
Predicted your wants
Arranged products perfectly
Ensured no stockouts

They are invisible but essential, the quiet architects of convenience.

Without them, shelves go empty, stores collapse, and customers walk away.

MODULE III — The Modern Retail Strategist: The Quiet Thinker

Forget the idea of "stacking shelves."

A retail strategist is a planner, analyst, designer, negotiator, and trend interpreter.

What They Actually Do

AREA	STRATEGIC ROLE
Global Sourcing	Find suppliers in Turkey, China, Kenya, Vietnam
Trend Prediction	Spot what customers will want before they want it
Visual Merchandising	Design displays that influence buying
Store Layout	Arrange products to increase sales

AREA	STRATEGIC ROLE
Buying Decisions	Protect profits through smart purchasing
Customer Insight	Know what sells fast, what gathers dust, what sparks joy

They understand customers deeply.
They sit at the center of supply chains.
They bridge factories and families.

Many CEOs and brand managers began here — not because it was glamorous, but because it taught everything: human behavior, sales psychology, trend analysis, negotiation, trust-building.

Watch closely.
You won't stay at the counter.
You will grow. Rise. Build.

MODULE IV — The Inner Frame: Temperament, Integrity, Discipline

Retail strategy is not only skill, but it is a character.

The Retail Strategist's Inner Frame

TRAIT	WHY IT MATTERS
Curiosity	Trends change fast — you must stay ahead
Integrity	Pricing, stock, suppliers — honesty builds trust
Discipline	Inventory, orders, data — consistency wins

TRAIT	WHY IT MATTERS
Kindness	Customers return to people who treat them well
Quick Thinking	Fix problems immediately
Reliability	Stores depend on you daily

These traits turn a "shop worker" into a strategic force.

MODULE V — Honest Tension: Real Work, Real Rewards

The work is meaningful, but not easy.

The Challenges

Crowded, warm stores

Long days during peak seasons

Starting salaries of GH¢800–1,500

Fast-changing trends

Costly mistakes

But purpose teaches discernment, not exhaustion.

A clear-eyed strategist:

Chooses stores that value ideas

Learns Shopify, inventory apps, trend tools

Grows displays and orders

Negotiates based on results

Leaves places that refuse to grow

THE MR. Kwame Story

He needs a store manager.

Candidate A: Business graduate with a diploma and internships

Candidate B: Retail strategist with no degree who doubled sneaker sales, found better suppliers, and knows customers personally

The strategist wins.

Why?

Results + trust + wisdom > certificates.

The world overlooks shelf-arrangers.

But they arrange futures.

MODULE VI — Every Store Is A Business School

Supermarkets, boutiques, electronics shops, and online stores all teach real business.

The Hidden Teams Behind Every Store

TEAM	ROLE
Buying Team	Selects products, negotiates prices, predicts trends
Visual Team	Designs displays that attract customers
Digital Team	Runs Instagram, TikTok, online stores
Customer Team	Builds loyalty, solves problems
Stock Team	Maintains flow and prevents shortages
Finance Team	Tracks money, budgets, profits

Even small stalls follow these patterns.

Every role shapes success.

MODULE VII — The Buyer: Culture-Shaper

The buyer decides what appears on shelves and screens.

They:

Track global and local trends

Choose sneakers, gadgets, clothes

Budget with instinct and data

Negotiate with factories and brands

Your sneakers exist because a Ghanaian buyer studied TikTok, supplier catalogs, and customer feedback.

One decision can shift sales, support makers, and shape neighborhoods.

Buyers blend math, culture, curiosity, and instinct.

They don't just stock, they create.

MODULE VIII — Path: Skills, Heart, Global Reach

SHS Start

STEP	ACTION
1	Finish SHS strong (Business, ICT, Elective Maths)
2	Learn Shopify, Canva, Google Trends (3–6 months)
3	Practice in family shops, stalls, or online

Skills Evolution

YESTERDAY	TODAY (2026)
Manual ordering	Alibaba, Jumia, Temu mastery
Shelf stacking	Instagram/TikTok visual displays
Price guessing	Data-driven predictions
Cash counting	Mobile money + POS systems

Heart That Wins

- Curiosity
- Honesty
- Kindness
- Quick thinking
- Reliability

These build trust, and trust builds careers.

Career Ladder

Stock Assistant

Retail Strategist

Store Manager

Category Manager

Supply Chain Specialist

Entrepreneur / Brand Owner

Accra kids now supply London, Nairobi, Dubai — digital tools make it possible.

FINAL WORD — The Shelf That Feeds Nations

Retail strategy is not "just arranging."

It is:

Creativity that turns boxes into wishlists
Service that meets needs before they're spoken
Business that connects farms to tables
Influence that shapes choices quietly
Opportunity hidden behind counters

The world needs retail strategists who are:
Curious enough to spot trends
Honest enough to earn endless trust
Creative enough to make shelves sing
Kind enough to serve joyfully
Smart enough to grow profits
Brave enough to build futures

Step confidently.
Shelves become strategy.
Stocking becomes success.
Daily work builds generations.
You did not dream small.
You dreamed wisely and became essential.
Purpose moves gently.
Purpose chooses quietly.
What will yours shape?

SEAMSTRESS & TAILOR EMPIRE

The Silent Architects of Identity

MAKOLA MARKET BREATHED WITH COLOR. AMA watched Abena, a young seamstress, guide vibrant kente beneath a humming machine. Kojo stood nearby, studying Master Kwame as he drafted a groom's suit with geometric precision.

Abena whispered, "She sees the bride before she cuts the cloth." Kwame told Kojo, "Every sleeve angle carries family legacy."

A garment is never just fabric. It is dignity for brides, belonging for students, authority for leaders, identity for nations. From blue-jean empires to global fashion houses, your needle writes history.

Gen Alpha truth: Your hands build clothing dynasties.

MODULE I — Jacob Davis: The Tailor Who Riveted A $100b Empire

1870, Reno. Laborers' trousers tore daily in mines and railroads. Jacob Davis Latvian tailor—listened.

His solution: Reinforced denim with copper rivets. Strengthened stress points. Built trousers that survived hard labor.

1873: Partnered Levi Strauss. Patent #139,121. Today: Levi's® $100B empire still uses Davis's rivets.

Lesson: Tailors don't mend trousers. They build workwear civilizations.

MODULE II — Barthélemy Thimonnier: The Seamstress Who Invented Factories

1830, France. Hand-sewing couldn't meet military demand. Thimonnier invented first practical sewing machine—200 stitches per minute.

Twice, mobs destroyed his factory. Twice, he rebuilt. His invention birthed the modern garment industry.

Lesson: Seamstresses don't hem dresses. They birth mass-production empires.

MODULE III — Yaa Mensah, Kojo Asare & Zalia Yakubu: Ghana's Rising Needle Empire

YAA Mensah (Accra): Started with GH¢650 + scraps. 2026: Bridal boutique, 18 seamstresses, GH¢7,200 monthly.

Kojo Asare (Kumasi): Learned suit-drafting from Master Kwame. 2026: School-uniform chain, 22 tailors, GH¢8,400 monthly.

Zalia Yakubu (Tamale): Smock apprentice at 15. Age 23: Exports custom smocks to UK & Canada.

Mary Brown's lesson: Store dress $32.50 → Homemade $11 = $100 value. Truth: Skill outperforms certificates. Mastery outlasts degrees.

MODULE IV — Ghana's Clothing Goldmines

Annual demand: 1.8M school uniforms, 900K choir robes, 2.4M wedding gowns & suits, 500+ corporate kente contracts, national sports kits.

Machines can sew. No machine understands Ghanaian curves, kente symbolism, or cultural fit. Your hands do.

MODULE V — SHS Subjects → Needle Mastery

SKILL	SUBJECT	FORMULA
Pattern	Geometry	Chest–waist–hip ratios
Fabric	Arithmetic	Meters × width = yield
Pricing	Business	(Labor + materials) × profit
Cutting	Physics	Bias grain × stretch control
Color	Art	Warm/cool balance

Truth: Math + science + creativity = sewing empire.

MODULE VI — Tools Arsenal (Gh¢5,800 Startup)

- Industrial machine (GH¢3,200)
- Overlocker (GH¢850)
- Adjustable dress form (GH¢420)
- Tailor's shears (GH¢85)
- French curve set

- Pattern paper + weights
- Sleeve board + pressing ham
- Micro-serrated scissors
- Kente loom adapter

Tools amplify genius they don't replace it.

MODULE VII — The 10 Eternal Stitching Laws

1. Measure thrice, cut once (fabric religion)
2. Grainline must be true (drape absolute)
3. Press every seam (95% quality)
4. French seams for luxury (invisible perfection)
5. Staystitch curves (shape keeper)
6. Always test with muslin (client perfection)
7. Respect kente bias (Ghana signature)
8. Deliver on time (integrity law)
9. Clean machine daily (tool commandment)
10. Sew for generations (legacy ethic)

MODULE VIII — Career Path: JHS → Empire

LEVEL	TIME	ROLE	INCOME	MILESTONE
1	6–12 mo	Uniforms	GH¢650 –1,400	Portfolio
2	1–3 yrs	Bridal/ market	GH¢2,800 –6,200	Reputation
3	3–5 yrs	Lead 12–20	GH¢9,500 –18K	Motorbike
4	5+ yrs	Boutique chain	GH¢25 –55K+	Multiple shops

Proof: Yaa, Kojo, Zalia—all under 25.

MODULE IX — Global Fashion Careers For Gen Alpha

Sewing opens doors to: Costume design (film, theater), textile technology (fabric innovation), pattern engineering (3D software), sustainable fashion (zero-waste), fashion merchandising (global brands), couture design (luxury houses), fashion tech (AI patterning, 3D scanning).

Your needle is a passport.

MODULE X — Sustainability: Sewing That Saves The Earth

Fashion pollutes more than aviation. Gen Alpha must lead change: Upcycle old garments, zero-waste cutting patterns, natural dyes (indigo, shea), fabric recycling systems, slow fashion principles.

Sewing creates. Sewing conserves.

MODULE XI — Pricing, Contracts & Client Mastery

1 tailor failure: Poor client management. Elite rules: 1. 50% deposit upfront (materials secured) 2. Written timeline (deadline protected) 3. Price by complexity (GH¢25 uniform vs GH¢1,200 bridal) 4. 20% overbooking buffer 5. Referral incentives (one bride = 5 clients)

Sample contract: "GH¢600 bridal gown. GH¢300 deposit today. Balance at first fitting. Delivery: Saturday 3pm. Late penalty: GH¢50/day."

Truth: Your word binds stronger than thread.

MODULE XII — Peak Seasons Goldmine

SEASON	PRODUCT	VOLUME	REVENUE
Easter	Choir robes	00 × GH¢85	GH¢17K
Schools	Uniforms	1,500 × GH¢25	GH¢37.5K
Weddings	Bridal	45 × GH¢1,200	GH¢54K
Corporate	Kente suits	120 × GH¢650	GH¢78K

4 months = year's income.

MODULE XIII — God: The Divine Seamstress

Scripture reveals craftsmanship: Genesis 3:21 God clothed Adam & Eve, Exodus 28 Priestly garments, exact measurements, Psalm 139 "Knit together in the womb," Ephesians 4 Body "joined perfectly together."

Your craft mirrors divine order. Your stitches echo creation.

MODULE XIV — The Cultural Weight Of Ghanaian Sewing

Ghanaian sewing carries: Kente symbolism (clan identity), smock heritage (Northern pride), kaba & slit elegance (feminine power), funeral cloth dignity (honor the dead), naming ceremony identity (welcome the newborn), school uniform belonging (1.8M united).

You preserve culture stitch by stitch.

FINAL WORD — Generation Alpha, Rise

Raise your right hand: "My hands craft dignity. My stitches preserve culture. My word is iron. Kente over couture. 2.4M weddings over runway dreams. Needle Empire over fashion school. Yɛn Ara Asaase Ni."

Jacob Davis riveted $100B Levi's. Thimonnier birthed factories. Ama, Kojo, Zalia built empires before 25.

Your needle can clothe nations. Your creativity shapes identity. Your discipline builds dynasties. Which empire will you stitch first?

WHEEL EMPIRE: PILOT– TRAIN–TRUCK–TAXI

The Silent Architects of Movement

IMAGINE THIS. AN AIRPORT ANYWHERE IN THE WORLD Accra, Lagos, Nairobi, New York, London. A young traveler steps off a flight, pauses at the aircraft door, and says to the pilot: "Thank you for bringing us home safely." The pilot smiles: "I planned your safe landing before we left."

Imagine this. A railway yard at dawn Tema, Johannesburg, Chicago, Delhi. A teenager watches a freight engineer sound the horn as cocoa, steel, grain, or fuel rolls toward the port. The engineer says: "These rails carry the nation's prosperity."

Imagine this. A major highway Tamale, Mombasa, Texas, Dubai. A young fleet owner climbs into the lead truck of a large convoy. He checks the manifest and radios his team: "Our wheels feed countless families."

These scenes are not history. They are possibility. They

are allegory. They are the future Generation Alpha can build anywhere in the world.

One truth remains: Transportation is the heartbeat of every nation. SHS/JHS graduates your hands move the world.

MODULE I — Bessie Coleman: First Black Woman Pilot

1920, Chicago. Bessie Coleman, a manicurist, hears airplanes overhead. Every U.S. flight school rejects her: "No Blacks. No women."

She refuses to stay grounded. Learns French at night. Saves every coin. Sails across the Atlantic. Trains with the Caudron Brothers in France.

1921: She earns an international pilot's license the first Black woman aviator in the world. She returns home a stunt-flight legend.

Truth: Pilots conquer skies that once said "no."

MODULE II — Christine Gonzalez Aldeis: First Female Train Engineer

1970s, Santa Fe Railway. Freight crews are almost entirely male. Christine Aldeis begins as a brakeman coupling cars in freezing nights, mastering air brakes and signals. She becomes the first woman locomotive engineer on a U.S. Class I railroad.

Truth: Train drivers connect continents, not just cars.

MODULE III

Lillie Drennan: First Female Truck Empire

1920s, Texas. Deaf. Doubted. Dismissed. Lillie Drennan demands a commercial driving test. She passes under scrutiny. She builds Drennan Truck Line America's first licensed female-owned freight company.

Truth: Truckers don't just drive they move nations.

MODULE IV — Jack Black: Taxi Safety Pioneer

1900s, London. Motor cabs are dangerous. Streets are chaotic. Jack Black drives decades accident-free. He helps establish: The Knowledge of London (thousands of streets), Vehicle inspections, Licensing standards.

His work becomes the foundation of the world-class London Black Cab system.

Truth: Taxi drivers build trust, not just fares.

MODULE V — Why The Whole World Depends On Transportation

Every profession stands on the shoulders of transportation: Teachers cannot teach if textbooks never arrive. Doctors cannot save lives if medicine stays stuck in warehouses. Traders cannot sell goods if trucks do not move. Farmers cannot earn income if crops cannot reach the market. Politicians cannot govern if citizens cannot travel to vote. Factories cannot operate if raw materials do not reach their gates. Students cannot study abroad if planes do not fly. Businesses cannot grow if goods cannot cross borders.

Transportation is the invisible foundation beneath every visible success.

MODULE VI — Transport Goldmines (Global + Africa)

Millions of taxi passengers in major cities. Millions of tons of freight moving through ports worldwide. Hundreds of thousands of air passengers every month. Railway revival across Africa, Asia, and Europe. Fuel distribution routes powering entire economies.

No drone understands African roads, Asian monsoons, European winters, or American highways the way human hands do.

MODULE VII — SHS Subjects → Wheel Power

SKILL	SUBJECT	APPLICATION
Navigation	Geography	Chart routes, read terrain
Load	Physics	Balance weight & stability
Fuel	Arithmetic	Plan efficiency & range
Timing	Business	Coordinate deliveries
Safety	Chemistry	Maintain brakes & fluids

Truth: Knowledge becomes precision. Precision becomes empires.

MODULE VIII — Startup Tools (Per Profession)

Pilot: flight computer, headset, charts. Truck: GPS, scales, load tracker. Train: brake tester, route maps. Taxi: taximeter, ride-hailing app, dashcam.

Tools obey disciplined hands.

MODULE IX — 10 Eternal Transport Laws

1. Pre-trip inspection
2. Perfect load center
3. Weather check multiple times
4. Fuel calculation first
5. Manifest verified
6. Brake every hill
7. Local knowledge > GPS
8. Deliver on schedule
9. Logbook daily
10. Drive for legacy

MODULE X — Career Paths: Each Vehicle Its Ladder

(Timelines vary by country; check local requirements.)

Pilot Path: Student → Co-pilot → Captain → Trainer

Train Engineer Path: Apprentice → Junior driver → Class I engineer → Senior engineer

Truck Fleet Path: Apprentice → Solo driver → Fleet manager → Fleet owner

Taxi Path: Apprentice → Licensed driver → Mentor → Fleet owner

Truth: Every transport path has its own pace. Skill and patience matter more than uniform timelines.

MODULE XI — Wheel Empire vs Office

TRANSPORT	OFFICE
Millions served	Papers processed
Daily visible impact	Work unseen
Skills protect lives	Degrees dusty
Recession-resistant	Layoff risk

Truth: Transport moves nations. Offices move documents.

MODULE XII — Contracts & Safety

Secure deposits. Verify manifests. Combine GPS with local knowledge. Maintain logs. Keep insurance current.

Check local regulations for examples and best practices.

MODULE XIII — Peak Seasons

Christmas: passenger surge. Harvest: crop transport. Easter: pilgrimages. Imports: container traffic.

Truth: Timing creates opportunity. Study local patterns.

Final Word

Say this in your heart with your hands lifted up "My hands steer nations. My wheels lift dreams. My word is my route. I honor safety. I build trust. I move the world forward."

Bessie broke barriers. Christine mastered rails. Lillie conquered roads. Jack built standards.

Now it is your turn. The world calls: Airlines need pilots. Ports need truckers. Railways need engineers. Cities need taxi masters.

Your wheel awaits. Which dynasty will you drive first?

15

CHOOSE WITH CARE

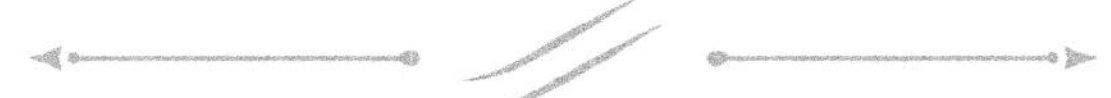

MODULE I — Life's Silent Thieves: The Cost Of Borrowed Dreams

MANY YOUNG ADULTS WAKE AT DAWN AND dress for jobs their parents chose. Mama dreamed of a doctor's white coat, her own dreams left undone. Papa imagined a lawyer's wig; his farm toil too dusty. Friends flock to banks; prestige glimmers brighter than joy. Money calls: "Doctor! Engineer!" Titles dazzle.

They leave home heavy. Return heavier. Jobs secured, but souls adrift. Contentment flees. Stress, burnout, and resentment grow silently.

Whatever job you choose, as long as it serves society, it should lift, not chain. God gave your fire, not theirs. Happiness in work is not optional. Work consumes most waking hours; it should energize your soul, not stifle it.

MODULE II — Parental Pressure Vs Personal Truth

Hank Azaria graduated from Tufts University with honors in drama in 1985 because his parents demanded it. He walked at graduation two credits short, completed at UCLA. Hated scripted stage work. Bartended in New York and was fired on Day One. Broke in Los Angeles, stumbled into voice acting genius:

- Moe Szyslak
- Chief Wiggum
- Comic Book Guy

35+ years on The Simpsons. Five Emmys. $80M career. 2016 commencement: "Ignore instincts at your peril."

Lesson: Parental pressure creates a wrong life. Authenticity produces excellence.

Vera Wang earned Sarah Lawrence honors in 1968. Parents wanted law. Tried, hated, pivoted. From Vogue fashion journalism to a bridal empire at 40. $700M brand serving royalty, celebrities.

Lesson: Prestige cannot replace purpose. Never too late to pivot.

MODULE III — The Misfit Problem: When Work Feels Wrong

Jack Williams drifted: carpentry, janitor, farm labor. Never stayed long. Never discovered strengths. By 33, fired five times in two years. By 54, moved trunks in train shed, grateful to survive.

Lesson: Misalignment destroys potential. Wrong reasons create quiet frustration.

Reflection Questions:

1. Whose dream am I carrying?
2. What drains vs energizes me?
3. Do I feel growth, joy, purpose?

MODULE IV — Why So Many Are Miserable At Work

Surveys: 50–75% workers have the wrong occupation. Why?

Wrong Choices:

- Parents
- Friends
- Prestige
- Money
- Fear/pressure

Right Choices:

- Joy
- Aptitude
- Temperament
- Calling
- Purpose

Misalignment: restlessness, boredom, frustration, low performance

Alignment: energy, creativity, growth, excellence, fulfillment

MODULE V — How To Choose With Care: Reflective Framework

Career choice = knowing yourself.

4. **Study Health:** Weak lungs → avoid dust. Heart issues → no heavy lifting. Anxiety → avoid crowds.

5. **Study Mind:** Abstract → law/ministry. Mechanical → ICT/carpentry. Social → sales/hospitality.

6. **Study Temperament:** Quiet/crowds? Routine/variety? Alone/people? Precision/creativity?

7. **Study Interests:** Enjoy when unwatched? Drawing, fixing, writing, cooking, helping?

8. **Study Adaptability:** Learn fast? Handle change? Stay consistent?

9. **Study Values:** What matters most? Life/impact desired?

10. **Study Future:** Pays? Growth? Identity alignment?

Rate: Low/Medium/High. Find patterns.

MODULE V-A — Career Choice Chart For Generation Alpha

Career Choice Framework

DOMAIN	STEP/ ACTION	WHY MATTERS	EXAMPLE
Self-Reflection	Identify strengths/ interests	Know talents	List subjects/ hobbies/ skills
	Temperament /personality	Avoid misfits	Patient? Creative? Intro/extro?
	Values/ passions	Align with purpose	What excites mornings?
Exploration	Research occupations	Understand options	Libraries, career guides
	Observe professionals	See real work	Shadow barber/ nurse/ mechanic
	List pros/cons	Realistic comparison	Income/ hours/ training/ stress
Mentorship	Seek mentors	Experience wisdom	Teachers/ pastors/ artisans
	Targeted questions	Avoid surprises	"Hardest parts? Key skills?"

DOMAIN	STEP/ ACTION	WHY MATTERS	EXAMPLE
Experimentation	Intern/ volunteer/ apprentice	Test before commit	Shop/clinic/ project assistant
	Small projects	Build skills	Sell water/ repair phones
	Reflect experiences	Adjust reality	What felt rewarding?
Decision Making	Narrow top 2–3 options	Focus energy	Strengths/ interest/ goals
	Intentional choice	Commit growth/joy	Write path + reasons
	Plan training	Prepare success	Classes/ apprentice-ships
Growth	Continue learning	Skills evolve	Workshops/ reading
	Build resilience	Handle challenges	Weekly progress reflection
	Align service	Meaningful work	"How helps community?"

Happiness + growth + impact = career worth pursuing.

MODULE VI — Career Pivot Flowchart

WRONG PATH? (Pressure/Prestige/Fear)

   ↓ NO

[JOY + GROWTH + SERVICE]

   ↓ YES

PAUSE & REFLECT (Modules I–V)

   ↓

TEST PIVOT (Shadow/Experiment/Mentors)

   ↓

CHOOSE AUTHENTICALLY (Chart + Oath)

   ↓

THRIVE (Energy + Excellence + Impact)

Pivot early like Azaria/Wang for lifelong freedom.

MODULE VII — Oath Of The Aligned Career

"I choose with care.
I choose honesty.
I choose courage.
I choose self-knowledge.
I choose a path fitting my hands, mind, and heart.
I choose life, I wake happy to live."

FINAL DECREE

Azaria ignored instincts and then listened. Wang chased prestige, then pivoted. Jack drifted too late.

Generation Alpha: Wrong reasons = quiet frustration. Right reasons = joy, excellence, peace.

Your Charge: Reflect. Pivot. Claim joyfully. Work happily. Serve holy. Live free.

16

GETTING HIRED

MODULE I — The Hidden Edge: Show Up To Stand Out

EMPLOYERS DON'T HIRE PAPER. THEY HIRE YOU FOR your grit, glow, and fit. Ten CVs stack for chair factory foreman. Then you walk in: steady eyes, callused hands from tro-tro repairs, voice commanding respect. Letters fade. You ignite.

In-person trumps apps every time. Your presence sells what pixels can't. God shaped your spark, let it shine.

MODULE II — Clear The Gate: Working Papers First

Underage or in school? Secure permits: parental consent, school approval, age proof. Ghana? Free SHS offices or labor desks for apprenticeships in carpentry, mechanics, and ICT.

Ask principal/pastor: "What's required?" Rules don't bind; they build futures.

Lesson: Obey early. Doors fling wide.

MODULE III — Nail The Interview: Three Fires To Light

Boss thinks: Is this my hire? Win with:

1. **SPARK INTEREST** — Smile real, stand tall, connect
2. **PROVE POWER** — Stories beat boasts: "Led shop fixes, zero breakdowns."
3. **IGNITE DESIRE** — "Your crew thrives with my hands."

Appearance Wins: Clean shirt, polished shoes, no scent overload. Spotless stenographer beat perfumed mess.

Prep Questions: Age? Skills? "Why leave last?" "Hobbies?" Answer bold: "Church repair club—fixed 50 bikes, served community."

End strongly: Thank warmly. Exit proud. No begging.

Mirror-practice now. Record. Refine.

MODULE IV — Letter Warrior: Cut Through The Stack

No walk-in? Write fiercely. Crisp 8x11 bond, typed clean. Goals: Stand out, hook, prove, crave.

Weak: "Saw your ad..." (Sleepy)

Fire: "Doubled salon sales 18% via client trust. Let's talk."

Unsolicited? Target mechanics shops, markets. Fewer people, your choice.

Each letter plants a seed. Precision sows; courage reaps; God harvests.

MODULE V — Job Hunt Framework

1. **PREP:** Papers, Polish, Pitch

    Gather permits, CV, and stories. Iron kitenge, polish shoes. Pitch: "Led church fixes—50 bikes saved."

2. **HUNT:** Person First, Letters Next

    Walk workshops. Type specifics: "20% workflow boost—your team next?" Seek unadvertised doors.

3. **SHINE:** Interview Fire

    Spark (smile, eyes). Prove (stories). Ignite (value). Neat, confident.

4. **SEAL:** Thank-Yous & Lessons

    Note: "Grateful—ready now." Journal nos for yeses.

MODULE V-A — Job Hunt Chart For Generation Alpha

Job Hunt Framework

DOMAIN	STEP/ ACTION	WHY MATTERS	GHANA EXAMPLE
Prep	Get papers	Unlock legal doors	Free SHS/ labor office
	Groom sharp	Impress first	Ironed kitenge/ clean kicks

DOMAIN	STEP/ ACTION	WHY MATTERS	GHANA EXAMPLE
	Craft stories	Prove edge	"50 tro-tros repaired"
Apply	Walk in	Face > paper	Accra workshops
	Type bold letters	Rise in piles	"Sales up 30%—your turn?"
	Unsolicited targets	Choose boss	Salons/ mechanics mail
Interview	Spark interest	Hook hearts	Eye contact/ firm shake
	Show skills	Deliver proof	"100 fixes, zero complaints"
	Build desire	They chase you	"Your crew needs my fire"
Follow	Thank & track	Lock wins	"Grateful— ready now" note
	Reflect nos	Fuel yeses	Journal pivots
Mindset	Serve community	Joy forever	"How lifts Ghana?"

Tip: Shadow plumber today—land lifetime trade tomorrow.

MODULE VI — Job Hunt Flowchart

READY? (Papers?)

    ↓NO → SECURE (School/Labor)

    ↓YES

HUNT (Person/Letter/Unsolicited)

    ↓

INTERVIEW (Spark/Prove/Desire)

    ↓YES → HIRED! Serve Joyfully

    ↓NO → PAUSE & REFLECT → PIVOT

Trace weekly. Nos build empires.

MODULE VII — Oath Of The Job Hunter

"I hunt with courage.
Present with polish.
Prove with stories, spark with heart.
Serve with soul.
Claim work fitting hands, heart, and home.
Lift self and society skyward."

Final Decree

Chair foreman won sans degrees by paint mastery, quiet command. Azaria voiced Simpsons gold from bar rags. Wang gowned queens from law dread.

Gen Alpha: Half-hearted hunts yield half-lives. Purposeful ones? Joy, growth, glory.

Charge: Prep. Shine. Serve holy. Thrive free.

17

LEVELING UP IN THE WAITING

*How to Build Strength, Skills, and Identity
Before the Job Arrives*

*For Generation Alpha in Ghana and
Across the Globe*

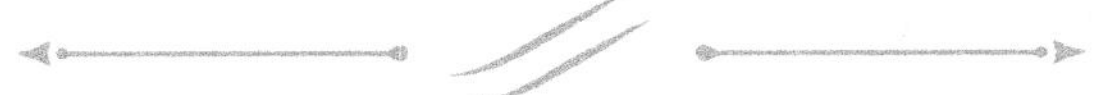

MODULE I — The Silent Season No One Posts About

GRADUATION: PHOTOS, APPLAUSE, GOWNS, CELEBRATION.
Next day: home. Refreshing emails. Job boards. Careful smiles for
relatives.

Across Ghana, Kenya, Nigeria, the UK, Canada, and the US,
millions of young adults share this season. A Kumasi graduate
helps chop bar. Nairobi diploma holders queue endlessly. A
Toronto student scrolls LinkedIn at 2 a.m. Lagos youth drives
Uber between interviews.

Everyone finished something. Finishing doesn't guarantee beginning.

Before the world gives contract, life shapes capacity.

Waiting is not punishment. It is positioning.

MODULE II — Charles Young Lesson: Free Time Is Your Future

Charles Young: 5 years at Atlas Steel. Expected promotion. Didn't get it.

Manager asked: "What time did you go to bed last night?"

Work hours are disciplined. Leisure hours wasted: movies, cards, joy rides, drifting weekends.

Income: $7,500. Savings: $25. Debt: $150.

The job wasn't a problem. Evenings were.

Changed: joined the gym, met promoted colleague Earl Wilson. Studied habits: reading, budgeting, exercise, skill-building.

One year later: promoted.

Lesson: Free time is an investment account. Poverty pushes movement. Idleness convinces one to stay the same.

MODULE III — Global Reality

Job markets are tight. Industries shifting. Technology replacing roles. Companies restructuring.

Waiting = normal. How you wait shapes who you become.

MODULE IV — Real Enemy: Unstructured Time

Unemployment is not the greatest threat. Unstructured time is.

Without structure, free hours become:

- anxiety
- comparison
- overthinking
- scrolling
- boredom
- wasted weeks
- wasted years

Time without direction erodes confidence.

MODULE V — Productive Leisure: Secret Weapon

Leisure = raw material.

Used wisely → strength, skill, clarity, creativity, opportunity, identity

Used carelessly → regret, stagnation, self-doubt

Question: "What are you doing with unsupervised hours?"

MODULE VI — Five Pillars For Powerful Waiting

Waiting Season Pillars

PILLAR	ACTION	OUTCOME
1. Body	Exercise daily	Discipline, energy, resilience
2. Mind	Read/courses/ tutorials	Knowledge compounds

PILLAR	ACTION	OUTCOME
3. Skills	Learn: coding/sewing/marketing	Options create freedom
4. Network	Mentors/artisans/leaders	Opportunities through people
5. Character	Patience/discipline/maturity	Success longevity

Skills create options. Character sustains them.

MODULE VII — Hobby Advantage

Hobbies build: creativity, confidence, community, identity.

Simple interest → side income → full career → brand → breakthrough.

What would you do with one free afternoon, no pressure? That clue matters.

MODULE VIII — Daily Structure Blueprint

Unemployment Daily Schedule

Morning (6-12):

- Wake early
- Exercise 30 min
- Read 20-30 min
- Apply 2-5 jobs
- Practice 1 skill

Afternoon (12-6):

- Volunteer/assist
- Network 1 person
- Personal project

EVENING (6-10):

- Reflect/journal
- Plan tomorrow
- Learn something new

Weekly:

- Track progress
- Update CV
- Build portfolio
- Review goals

Waiting → momentum.

MODULE IX — Time Budgeting

Budget time like money.

Track Your Hours:

- Sleep: 7-8 hrs
- Learning: 2 hrs minimum
- Exercise: 30-60 min
- Job apps: 1 hr
- Hobbies: 1-2 hrs
- Social: 1-2 hrs max
- Screen waste: Eliminate

Hours leak quietly. Reclaim. Redirect. Reinvest.

The future follows the calendar.

MODULE X — Waiting Season Oath

"I will not waste this season.
I use hours intentionally.
I grow quietly.
I strengthen body/mind.
I prepare for the opportunity.
This season builds me."

FINAL DECREE — When Not Working, You Are Becoming

The world sees unemployment. Growth still happens.

This season you are:

- Sharpening capacity
- Building identity
- Strengthening discipline
- Discovering strengths
- Preparing opportunity

Gen Alpha: Not pause. Training.

Use wisely. Grow intentionally. Prepare strategically.

When the door opens, walk through ready.

HOW TO KEEP A JOB

Stay, Grow, Rise: Become Indispensable

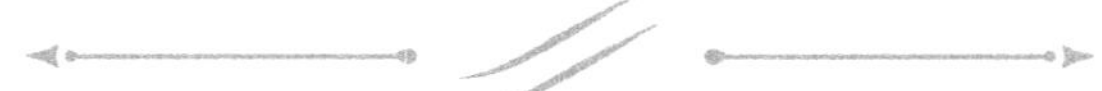

MODULE I — Hired Is Victory. Keeping It? The Real Work

POLISHED SHIRT, FIRM HANDSHAKE, DOOR OPENS. But staying? Character matters more than CVs. Employers hire potential. Keep discipline. Promote consistency.

Common pitfalls:

- Lateness
- Pride
- Tantrums
- Flakiness

Presentation gets you in. Consistency and growth keep you rising.

MODULE II — First 90 Days: Forge Your Reputation

Makola stall or multinational office—first 90 days whisper destiny.

Bosses notice: Punctual? Fast learner? Adaptable? Respectful? Finisher?

Perfection not required. Promise is.

What reputation are you building today?

MODULE III — Five Behaviors That Make You Irreplaceable

1. **Reliability** — Beat Ghana's lateness culture. Show early. Deliver daily. Your superpower.
2. **Teachability** — Pride blocks growth. Ask questions. Accept feedback. Your currency.
3. **Initiative** — See problems, solve, anticipate. Hidden leadership.
4. **Emotional Intelligence** — No snaps, gossip, sulking. Promotion fuel.
5. **Integrity** — No shortcuts. Let name be gold. Lifelong CV.

Which behavior will you sharpen today?

MODULE IV — Ghana Workplace Realities

Accra banks, Kumasi salons, Takoradi worksites: tough clients, jealous peers, slow systems. You cannot escape or conquer through growth.

Reacting hot? Respond professionally.

MODULE V — Promotion Formula

No begging. Follow pattern:

- Solve problems
- Ease stress
- Add value
- Build trust

Boss sleeps easier because of you → recognition/promotion follows.

MODULE VI — Seven Career Killers

Career Killers Table

Killer Impact

1. Chronic lateness Missed opportunities
2. Gossip/drama Broken trust
3. Laziness/fatigue Seen as unreliable
4. Boss conflicts Stunted growth
5. Sloppy hygiene Poor impression
6. Frequent borrowing Seen as unstable
7. Entitlement No promotions

Remove habits before they remove you.

MODULE VII — Conflict Mastery

Stay calm. Listen. Clarify. Apologize when needed. Escalate last.

Never fight publicly. Protect reputation. Protect the future.

MODULE VIII — Be Remembered Right

Greet warmly. Help freely. Learn quickly. Work diligently. Smile genuinely. Respect everyone.

Energy becomes a lasting brand.

MODULE IX — Daily Job Keeper Checklist

Daily Checklist

1. **Mind:** "How can I serve excellently today?"
2. **Body:** Clean, neat, fresh
3. **Tools:** Ready to perform
4. **Attitude:** Solutions, not complaints
5. **Value:** "What can I improve today?"

MODULE X — 90-Day Rise Flowchart

90-Day Rise Path

Day 1 → RELIABILITY (Arrive early, deliver steady)

Week 4 → TEACHABILITY (Ask, learn, adapt)

Month 3 → INITIATIVE (Solve, go extra)

↓ YES → INDISPENSABLE → Promotion Path

↓ CONFLICT? → CALM/RESPECT → RISE

↓ TIMING? → PATIENCE/CONSISTENCY → Opportunities

Track weekly. Consistency crowns commitment.

MODULE XI — Oath Of The Job Keeper

"I show up early.
I grow humble.
I serve excellently.
I rise disciplined.
I protect my name and work.
I become indispensable."

FINAL DECREE

Hired? Easy. Kept? Rare. Risen? Legendary.

Not the loudest, but steadfast wins. Azaria transformed bar jobs into Simpsons gold. Wang pivoted from law dread to royalty gowns.

Gen Alpha: Job is a platform, gym, stage for growth.

Charge: Excel. Build discipline. Rise consistently.

19

HOW TO EXIT A JOB WITH HONOR, STRATEGY, AND FUTURE POWER

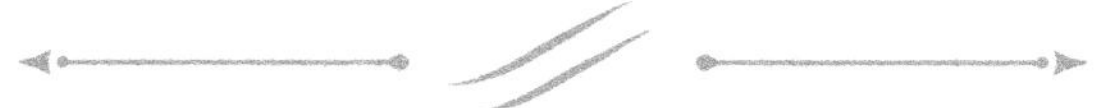

MODULE I — The Wisdom Of Timing

LEAVING A JOB IS NOT A FAILURE. IT IS TIMING. Discernment. Growth recognizing its next assignment. Some doors you outgrow. Some close by providence. Some you close yourself—gently, wisely, intentionally.

Every season has an expiration. Mature people know when the season speaks its last lesson.

How you leave determines: reputation, references, network, future access, and inner peace. Leaving well is not emotional. It is strategic.

Are you pushed by frustration or pulled by purpose?

MODULE II — The Four Signs The Season Has Ended

Not every difficulty means departure. Growth often hides in discomfort. Wisdom recognizes patterns.

1. **Growth Stopped** — No new skills, responsibility, intellectual stretching. Comfort becomes decay.
2. **Integrity Pressured** — Dishonesty, manipulation, ethical compromise. Never trade character for comfort.
3. **Health Deteriorating** — Chronic stress, anxiety, exhaustion. Job-destroying health charges too high.
4. **Verified Opportunity** — Real, stable, aligned—not emotion, rumor, wishful thinking.

Am I leaving at the right time or for the wrong reason?

MODULE III — The Law Of Reputation

People rarely remember first days. They remember last. Final attitude. Professionalism under pressure. Departure words. Transition handling.

Exit is a signature. Sign with excellence. Leave with honor, even if not treated perfectly.

Your name is an invisible passport. Protect it.

MODULE IV — Professional Exit Strategy

Disciplined professionals follow five principles:

1. **Decide In Silence** — Clarity needs no applause. Plan privately.
2. **Secure Next Step** — Unless safety/health/ethics demand immediate exit. Faith powerful. Preparation wisdom.

3. **Give Proper Notice** — 2 weeks entry, 1 month mid-level, longer senior.

4. **Write Dignified Letter** — "Grateful for growth. Ensure smooth transition."

5. **Finish Strong** — Complete assignments. Train successors. Leave better.

MODULE V — Seven Exit Errors That Follow Years

Exit Errors Table

Error Impact

1. No notice Unprofessional
2. Public criticism Burned bridges
3. Abandoned responsibilities No references
4. Taking property Legal trouble
5. Social media attacks Permanent record
6. Emotional outbursts Poor reputation
7. Recruiting out resentment Toxic label

Marketplace small. Reputation travels fast.

MODULE VI — Emotional Intelligence At Departure

Transitions stir: relief, fear, sadness, excitement, anger, uncertainty.

Maturity = discipline of expression. Feel fully. Speak carefully.

Control tone. Posture. Narrative. Strength is quiet.

MODULE VII — Exit Interview: Courage With Grace

Be honest. Specific. Constructive.

Say: "Grateful for learning. Transitioning toward growth/alignment."

No exaggeration. Attacks. Gossip.

Professionalism leaves doors unlocked.

MODULE VIII — Relationships Are Assets

Thank trainers, correctors, challengers, and believers.
Exchange contacts. Stay connected respectfully.
A former colleague may: recommend, hire, partner, or open doors.

Never leave relationships. Carry forward with gratitude.

MODULE IX — FINAL TWO WEEKS PROTOCOL

Two Weeks Exit Plan

Week 1:
- Document processes
- Clarify handovers
- Begin knowledge transfer

Week 2:
- Organize workspace
- Return property
- Finalize responsibilities

Final Day:

- Express appreciation
- Leave contact info
- Exit calmly

No bitterness. No chaos. Peaceful exits create powerful returns.

MODULE X — OATH OF THE HONORABLE EXIT

"I leave with dignity.
I protect my name.
I preserve relationships.
I complete faithfully.
I trust God ahead.
I walk without regret.
I rise with integrity."

FINAL DECREE — Power Of Leaving Well

Anyone quits. Few conclude excellently. Anyone walks away. Few transition with vision.

Leave well → marketplace remembers → trusted brand.

Gen Alpha: Exit, not chapter end. Opening of the next.

Close gently. Move strategically. Trust timing. Guard reputation. Step confidently.

The future prepares space for those who leave well.

20

WHEN LIFE TURNS – AND THE CLASSROOM IS OUT OF REAC

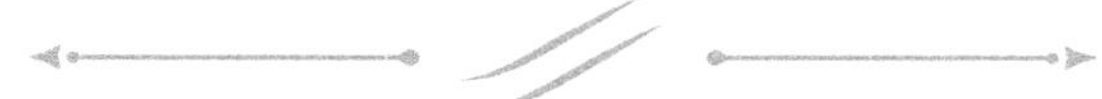

MODULE I — Life's Mystery Turns

LIFE IS A MYSTERY. WE PLAN CAREFULLY, ENROLL IN school, dream of certificates, and imagine steady progress. Yet life turns.

Providence is a wheel. One season lifts with opportunity. Next revolution sinks into hardship. Fees vanish. Illness visits. Family burdens arrive. Parent loses work. Classroom seat lost.

The greatest danger is not poverty. It is hopelessness—the belief that without certificates, destiny expires.

History refuses this conclusion.

MODULE II — Frederick Douglass: Learning When Forbidden

Born into slavery in 1818. Education illegal. Age 12, secretly learned the alphabet from white children. Taught himself: traced letters in dirt, read newspapers, mastered The Columbian Orator despite beatings.

1838 escaped slavery. Founded the North Star newspaper. The most photographed American of the century. U.S. Marshal, diplomat.

Books broke the chains law tried tightening.

MODULE III — Michael Faraday: School Ended Early

Left school at age 14; poverty required work. Bookbinder apprentice.

Read every scientific book bound. Copied lectures. Attended public talks. Curiosity became a classroom.

Age 22: a scientific assistant. Age 30: first electric motor. Age 40: electromagnetic induction—powers generators worldwide.

Declined titles/wealth. Pursued understanding.

MODULE IV — Emotional/Psychological/Social Reality

Classroom closure brings:

- Emotional: Shame, anxiety, "left behind" fear
- Psychological: Hopelessness, comparison, self-doubt
- Social: Peer pressure, family judgment, community whispers

Real obstacles. Heavy. Navigable.

Those acting with curiosity, discipline, and resilience rise emotionally, psychologically, and socially.

MODULE V — When Wheel Turns For You

Many young people began school but could not continue not due to laziness or rebellion, but because of life situations such as economic strain, family duties, tragedy, or health.
Classrooms close. Learning must not.

Education = gift. Teachers/structure matter. Learning > walls.

MODULE VI — Build When Classroom Distant
Self-Education Roadmap

1. Read daily (10-15 min): newspapers, tutorials, articles, books
2. Observe: mechanics, artisans, traders ask questions, take notes
3. Practice: hands/mind/heart trained daily
4. Mentors: barber, tailor, mechanic, pastor—learn experience
5. Volunteer: builds social skills, discipline, reputation
6. Small ventures: water sales, phone repair, food prep, digital services
7. Record progress: notebook/phone journal growth, failures, lessons
8. Body/mind care: sleep, nutrition, exercise
9. Attitude: patience, humility, persistence, positivity
10. Networks: peers, mentors, professionals

MODULE VII — Foundations Travel Everywhere

Enduring foundations:

- Health — first tool
- Curiosity — unlocks doors
- Apprenticeship — accelerates growth
- Discipline — outlasts talent
- Integrity — multiplies opportunity
- Service — value returns unseen

Foundations standing = paths open.

MODULE VIII — Psychological/Social Results

Roadmap delivers:

- Confidence: skill mastery builds self-belief
- Resilience: setbacks are less paralyzing
- Independence: self/mentor reliance vs failure fear
- Social respect: communities honor competence/service
- Opportunity: knowledge/skill/reputation open doors

MODULE IX — Word To Classroom Students

Cherish classroom. Respect it. Use fully.

Not in the classroom? Don't despise self. Don't surrender mind. Don't let comparison silence ambition.

Life nonlinear. The wheel turns. Today low, tomorrow lift. Next season tests again.

Constant: mind grows, character strengthens, faith sustains, discipline compounds, learning continues.

No interruption can cancel potential permanently.

MODULE X — How-To Chart For Generation Alpha

When Classroom Out Of Reach

DOMAIN	STEP/ ACTION	WHY MATTERS	EXAMPLE
Emotional	Recognize feelings	Awareness reduces stress	Journal fear/ shame/ anger
	Manage dis-appointment	Builds resilience	Breathing/ prayer when plans fail
	Celebrate small wins	Boosts confidence	Tutorial complete/ skill mastered
Social	Supportive relationships	Mentors guide growth	Observe artisan/ pastor, ask questions
	Communicate effectively	Opens doors	Share progress, seek feedback
	Serve others	Community respect	Market/ church/ neighbor-hood help
Practical Skills	Read daily	Expands knowledge	Newspa-pers/books/ online tuto-rials

	Hands-on practice	Mastery development	Phone repair/ cooking/ sewing
	Document learning	Tracks growth/ lessons	Notebook/ voice notes/ journal
	Small ventures	Entrepreneurship	Water sales/hair braiding/ digital
Daily Routines	Morning health	Energy/ focus foundation	Water/ breakfast/ exercise
	Learning goals	Consistency	30-60 min reading/ practice
	Evening reflection	Progress reinforcement	3 learned/1 improve
	Weekly review	Growth measurement	Test abilities/ plan next

Foundations strong → opportunity flows.

FINAL DECREE — The Wheel Will Turn Again

Douglass learned in secret dirt. Faraday studied while binding books. Both refused despair. Both built empires from interruption.

Generation Alpha's classroom closure is not the end of destiny.

Your Charge:

- Keep learning when walls close
- Build skills when seats vanish
- Forge character when fees disappear
- Trust providence when paths darken

The wheel turns for everyone.

When yours lifts again, be ready.

Not with certificates alone.

But with competence, curiosity, and courage.

Destiny rises with the prepared.

EPILOGUE

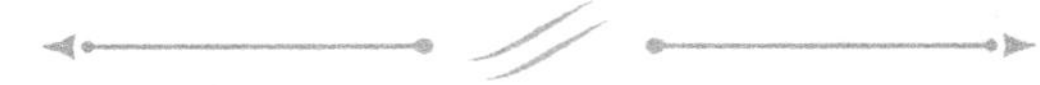

EVERY GENERATION INHERITS A QUESTION: WHAT makes a life honorable?

In an age that measures worth by rankings, followers, and titles, it is easy to believe that only a few paths are noble. Yet the truth is far older and far wiser than the noise of our moment.

Every school is worthy. Every honest career is honorable.

Whether a student studies in a classroom at Harvard University, Yale University, the University of Ghana, or a small school whose name does not appear on any global list, the dignity of learning remains the same. Education is not sanctified by prestige but by purpose. A mind that seeks truth with humility is no less noble in a village classroom than in the halls of the world's most celebrated universities.

The same is true of work.

Whether one becomes a president, a physician, a teacher, a farmer, an engineer, a gardener, an artisan, or any other servant of society, the calling itself is not what determines honor. What determines honor is the spirit with which the calling is fulfilled. A life becomes dignified when a person exhausts, with sincerity and diligence, the gifts and opportunities placed before them by God and by life.

No one needs to blush for an honest trade. The ancient words still hold their wisdom: "In the sweat of your face shall you eat bread." Genesis 3:19. Work is not a mark of shame; it is the signature of participation in creation itself. Laziness may bring embarrassment, but diligence never should. The worker who works faithfully in obscurity stands with as much dignity as the leader who speaks before nations.

For the world itself teaches this lesson if we are willing to observe it.

Creation is not uniform. It is magnificently diverse. The beauty of the world does not lie in sameness but in variety. Look at nature, and you will see that God, the Creator, delights in difference. Birds, beasts, fish, and insects fill the earth with forms that no single design could contain. Stones beneath our feet carry their own markings and veins. Gems sparkle each with a different light. The forests hold countless trees, plants, herbs, and flowers, each contributing its quiet part to the balance of life.

Even among the creatures of the sky, there is wonder in contrast. The tiny hummingbird flashes like a living jewel, while the eagle rises on immense wings to meet the storms above the clouds. Both belong to the same sky. Neither diminishes the other.

So it is with humanity.

It would be unwise for one Ghanaian, one American, or one Chinese person to say to another, "You are nothing because you cannot hold the same title I hold or have same work that I have." The world does not function through one office alone. Every society, like every kingdom, requires many kinds of service. Some lead nations. Some cultivate the land. Some build homes. Some teach minds. Some heal bodies. Some nurture families. Others guide communities quietly without recognition.

The greatness of a civilization lies not in the elevation of a few professions but in the faithful service of many.

History itself confirms this truth. Across the centuries, people from every walk of life have shaped the world. Leaders and workers alike have been instruments of change. Those who ploughed the soil and those who sailed the seas, those who forged tools and those who taught wisdom, have all contributed to the unfolding story of humanity.

There is, therefore, a profound dignity in honest work.

The rough hands of a farmer who feeds a nation carry no less honor than the polished hands of a president who governs it. The carpenter who shapes wood, the driver who moves people safely across distances, the teacher who awakens a child's curiosity, the nurse who watches through the night, the gardener who cultivates beauty from the soil, all share in the same sacred economy of service.

Even the Bible does not hesitate to record the names of cupbearers and servants alongside kings and prophets. The humble worker is not forgotten in the chronicles of faith or history.

Yet pride remains one of humanity's most persistent temptations.

In our age, achievements are broadcast instantly across digital platforms. Titles appear on profiles, announcements, and introductions. Accomplishments are displayed as badges of distinction. Society often treats certain careers as though they confer a higher form of humanity.

But dignity does not originate in titles.

There is a greater honor than prestige, a deeper distinction than reputation: the honor of serving humanity with integrity. It is an honor recognized not only by people but by heaven itself, an honor that angels would understand even if the world overlooks it.

And so a deeper question must always be asked:
Who truly distinguishes one person from another?
Who grants the opportunities, talents, and circumstances that shape a life?

However brilliant a person's abilities, however remarkable their opportunities, the ultimate source of those gifts lies beyond them. They are entrusted by God, not manufactured by humans. They are received, not self-created.

This truth has the power to silence pride.

For we are the work of a Creator's design. The excellence within us is not a reason for arrogance but a reason for gratitude. The recognition we receive should not inflate us but remind us of our responsibility to use what has been given wisely.

Work done well, no matter how ordinary it appears, is worthy of respect.

A nation may applaud its presidents and its scholars, but it cannot survive without its farmers, builders, cleaners, drivers, and countless others whose names rarely appear in public praise. Civilization rests upon the quiet fidelity of people who perform necessary tasks with integrity.

The measure of a life, therefore, is not where one studies or what title one carries. The measure is whether the work entrusted to them is done with diligence, humility, and service.

For Generation Alpha, the generation growing up in a world of rapid change, digital visibility, and global comparison, this truth is essential.

Do not let the world convince you that only certain paths are worthy.

Choose excellence wherever you are.
Honor the work before you.
Respect the callings of others.
Serve with integrity, whether the stage is large or small.

God, the Creator of this vast and varied world, has never limited dignity to a single road. Just as no two leaves are identical and no two stars shine with the same light, no two lives are meant to unfold in exactly the same way.

And that is not a flaw in the design.
It is the beauty of it.
The world is filled with marvels, and no two marvels are alike.

APPENDIX

PART I: FOUNDATIONS OF SKILLED WORK
(Chapters 1–4)

A. The Dignity of Skilled Trades

Work as Craft: Skilled trades combine knowledge, discipline, and practical intelligence.

Technical Mastery: Craftsmen apply mathematics, observation, and problem-solving.

Service to Society: Trades sustain daily life through housing, food, transport, and infrastructure.

B. Apprenticeship and Skill Formation

Apprenticeship Systems: Learning through hands-on practice under experienced masters.

Technical Training Pathways: TVET, NVTI, and technical institutes preparing skilled workers.

Lifelong Skill Development: Tradespeople continually refine knowledge and techniques.

C. Professional Character

Integrity in Craft: Honest work builds trust and long-term reputation.

Precision and Patience: Careful attention to detail prevents costly mistakes.

Reliability and Discipline: Consistency is the foundation of mastery.

PART II: MECHANICAL AND CONSTRUCTION TRADES
(Chapters 5–7)

A. Automobile Service

Applied Engineering: Vehicle repair integrates mechanical, electrical, and digital systems.

Diagnostic Skills: Technicians identify faults through testing equipment and system analysis.

Safety Responsibility: Accurate repairs prevent accidents and protect families.

B. Building Construction

Shelter as Infrastructure: Buildings provide the physical platforms where societies function.

Construction Trades: Masonry, carpentry, plumbing, electrical work, and steel fabrication.

Professional Pathways: Apprentice → specialist → foreman → contractor.

C. Carpentry and Woodcraft

Mathematics and Precision: Carpentry requires measurement, geometry, and structural understanding.

Wood Selection: Different timber types serve specific construction and furniture needs.

Cabinetry and Joinery: Advanced woodcraft producing durable structures and interiors.

PART III: ESSENTIAL SERVICE TRADES
(Chapters 8–10)

A. Electrical Systems

Power Distribution: Electricians install and maintain wiring systems in homes and cities.

Safety Protocols: Proper grounding and load management prevent electrical hazards.

Emerging Technologies: Solar systems and smart home installations.

B. Plumbing and Sanitation

Water Systems: Plumbers design and maintain clean water supply and drainage networks.

Public Health Role: Sanitation infrastructure protects communities from disease.

Maintenance and Repair: Diagnosing leaks, pressure issues, and pipe failures.

C. Painting and Surface Finishing

Surface Protection: Paint protects buildings from weather and structural decay.

Color and Design: Skilled painters contribute to aesthetics and visual identity.

Professional Preparation: Surface cleaning, priming, and finishing techniques.

PART IV: LAND, FOOD, AND ENVIRONMENT
(Chapters 11–13)

A. Farming and Agricultural Systems

Science-Based Agriculture: Soil testing, irrigation, and crop management increase productivity.

Agricultural Diversification: Combining crops, livestock, and value-added processing.

Food Security: Agriculture sustains national nutrition and economic stability.

B. Forestry and Environmental Stewardship

Forest Ecosystems: Forests regulate climate, water cycles, and biodiversity.

Timber and Non-Timber Products: Resources such as timber, honey, and medicinal plants.

Sustainable Management: Reforestation and conservation practices.

C. Animal Systems

Livestock Management: Poultry, cattle, goats, and dairy production.

Animal Health: Vaccination programs and hygiene practices.

Agricultural Enterprise: Farming as both science and business.

PART V: CREATIVE AND PERSONAL SERVICE TRADES
(Chapters 14–15)

A. Hair and Beauty Professions

Cultural Expression: Hairstyles and beauty practices reflect identity and heritage.

Personal Confidence: Beauty professionals restore dignity and self-esteem.

Career Progression: Apprentice → stylist → salon owner → brand developer.

B. Culinary Arts

Food as Culture: Cuisine reflects history, hospitality, and community traditions.

Kitchen Systems: Hygiene, budgeting, and ingredient management.

Entrepreneurial Opportunities: Restaurants, catering, and food production.

C. Sewing and Fashion

Garment Construction: Pattern drafting, fabric selection, and tailoring.

Fashion Identity: Clothing communicates cultural heritage and creativity.

Fashion Entrepreneurship: Tailoring shops, boutiques, and design houses.

PART VI: INDUSTRY, TRANSPORT, AND CAREER DEVELOPMENT
(Chapters 16–17)

A. Manufacturing and Production

Industrial Transformation: Converting raw materials into finished goods.

Manufacturing Sectors: Textiles, food processing, metal fabrication, and plastics.

Production Systems: Automation, assembly lines, and quality inspection.

B. Transportation Systems

Mobility Infrastructure: Air, rail, and road systems connecting societies.

Operational Skills: Navigation, safety management, and logistics coordination.

Professional Pathways: Drivers, pilots, engineers, and fleet managers.

C. Career Alignment and Growth

Choosing Work Wisely: Considering temperament, strengths, and long-term opportunity.

Professional Development: Building skills, reputation, and experience.

Career Progression: Mastery grows through discipline and continuous learning.

GLOSSARY

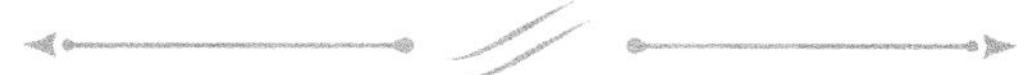

Skilled Trades and Craftsmanship

Apprenticeship: Learning a trade through supervised practical experience.

Joinery: Craft of connecting wooden pieces without nails or screws.

Diagnostics: Using tools and tests to identify mechanical or electrical faults.

Construction and Mechanical Systems

Masonry: Building structures using brick, stone, or concrete blocks.

Circuit Load: Total electrical demand placed on a power system.

Structural Frame: The main load-bearing skeleton of a building.

Agriculture and Environment

Soil Testing: Scientific analysis of soil nutrients and composition.

Reforestation: Planting trees to restore degraded forests.

Livestock Management: Caring for animals raised for food production.

Craft and Personal Services

Pattern Drafting: Creating templates used to cut fabric for garments.

Visual Merchandising: Designing displays that attract customers.

Food Safety: Practices preventing contamination during food preparation.

Career and Professional Growth

Skill Pathway: Career development built through vocational training.

Reputation Capital: Trust and credibility built through consistent conduct.

Career Alignment: Choosing work that fits one's temperament and abilities.

BIBLIOGRAPHY

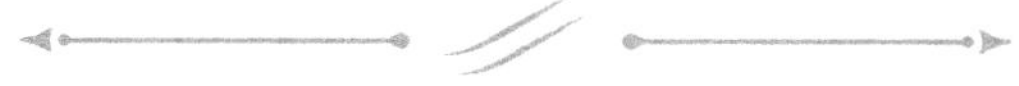

The Holy Bible. New King James Version (NKJV). Nashville, TN: Thomas Nelson.

https://www.biblegateway.com/versions/New-King-James-Version-NKJV-Bible/

United Nations Children's Fund (UNICEF). The State of the World's Children.

https://www.unicef.org/reports/state-of-worlds-children

World Health Organization (WHO). Global Reports on Adolescent and Youth Mental Health.

https://www.who.int/health-topics/adolescent-health

United Nations Educational, Scientific and Cultural Organization (UNESCO). Global Education Monitoring Reports.

https://www.unesco.org/gem-report

Ministry of Education (Ghana). Education Policy and Senior High School Reports.

https://moe.gov.gh

Ghana Education Service (GES). Secondary Education Statistics and Policy Reports.

https://ges.gov.gh

International Labour Organization (ILO). Youth Employment and Labour Market Reports.

[https://www.ilo.org/global/topics/youth-employment] (https://www.ilo.org/global/topics/youth-employment)

Publicly available global youth-culture observations and social media discourse (2015–2025), including widely accessible digital platforms and public discussions.

INDEX